Data Scientist
Bedside Manner

Developing the Skillset to Extract Business Value from Data Science and AI

Zacharias Voulgaris

Yunus Emrah Bulut

Technics Publications

Published by:

2 Lindsley Road, Basking Ridge, NJ 07920 USA
https://www.TechnicsPub.com

Edited by Riaz Howey
Cover design by Lorena Molinari

First Printing 2020
Copyright © 2020 by Zacharias Voulgaris and Yunus Emrah Bulut

ISBN, print ed.	9781634627832
ISBN, Kindle ed.	9781634627849
ISBN, ePub ed.	9781634627856
ISBN, PDF ed.	9781634627863

Library of Congress Control Number: 2020935539

Contents

CHAPTER 1

Data Science Landscape

The key differentiation between someone who thrives in data science and someone who merely survives, is the realization that ever since its inception, data science has been changing. Always adapting to the needs it was created to fulfill, data science has been a chameleon of sorts. Unlike statistics, which generally has a rigid mathematical framework based upon a series of assumptions on the underlying data, data science is very flexible in its structure and functionality, constantly developing new methods to tackle increasingly challenging problems.

The one thing that remains constant in data science is its mission: to provide hands-on solutions to these challenging problems using a combination of creativity and the scientific method.

This same creativity is responsible for the plethora of methods available in the data scientist's toolkit. These include techniques from math, programming, and, lately, advanced fields such as artificial intelligence (AI). Although many people still try to brand data science as statistics for business, in essence it is much more than that and nowadays you can be a competent data scientist without relying on statistics.

Over the past few years, data visualization has become a very popular methodology, and developing interactive graphics a sought-out skill. This is particularly the case when coupled with methods geared towards reducing the number of variables in the dataset, called *dimensionality reduction*. Additionally, niche methodologies like Artificial Neural Networks (ANNs) and Natural Language Processing (NLP) have led to specialization, especially in countries where the field has matured. The mindset of a good data scientist, however, has remained a constant factor across all these specializations, something we've explored in the book *Data Science Mindset, Methodologies, and Misconceptions*.

It's no doubt important to have the right mindset, which is a combination of the core qualities of a data scientist, coupled with an accurate perspective of the various methodologies and their use cases. In addition, it's equally important to understand that data science is much more than putting together scripts in Julia, Python, or some other programming language. Namely, it's essential to develop skills in these four areas:

1. **Applied math**: linear algebra, statistics, graph theory, and to some extent calculus (particularly for

AI). Even information theory and signal analysis have a place in data science, as well as any state-of-the-art research related to data processing, depending on the application domain.

2. **Programming**: Julia, Python, Scala, and R, and other languages, as well as all the libraries related to importing, formatting, and processing data efficiently. This includes some specialized packages for more advanced methodologies, such as for deep learning.

3. **Problem-solving**: modeling challenging problems in a mathematically comprehensive manner, figuring out effective and efficient strategies for deriving solutions to these problems using known methodologies like optimization, and creating comprehensible plots that describe and help solve the problem at hand.

4. **Business knowledge and understanding of how organizations work**: understanding how a modern organization functions, having a birds-eye view of data science projects, and productive relationships with stakeholders. Knowing the flow of information as well as the various means of communicating this information, along with processes and software that enable efficient

collaboration with other professionals in the organization.

Unfortunately, a disproportional amount of emphasis is given to the first three areas of data science, especially the first two, partly because it's easier for educators, and partly because of the warped view of a data scientist's role by some people involved in this field, usually indirectly.

A data scientist often tends to emphasize the most enjoyable aspects, or the ones she finds most relevant to her work, such as the methodologies applied or the application at hand. Naturally, things like machine learning, fancy dynamic plots, and AI methods come first, but beyond these, there is a lot more that is equally important for the data scientist role. There are things that many data scientists take for granted or don't feel confident enough to discuss. That's something we'll address in this book by exploring the business aspect of data science and how it relates to other parts of our field.

Business and data science

The business aspect of data science is what makes data science different from the more academic flavors of science. Even though data science has a research component to it, it is not geared towards publications, research grants, and conferences (although there are several noteworthy data science conferences out there). After all, the mission of data science is to provide value to an organization, something that is made possible by adhering to an organization's general workflow and mentality. Also, the organization can be a business or a non-profit since data science is quite versatile in its scope.

What constitutes value differs from organization to organization. For a research institute, for example, value is new knowledge and know-how, especially if it extends or supplements existing scientific knowledge. If you come up with something new in data science, be it a new algorithm, heuristic, or even a variant of an existing method, that's valuable. However, if the organization is concerned with predicting accurately next week's stock prices, an accurate predictive analytics system would be considered most valuable.

Other organizations may expect different things in order to accept a data scientist's work as valuable: well-written reports on the projects at hand, proper modeling of a complex business process, useful (actionable) insights based on client feedback, or any combination of these things.

Domain knowledge has always been important in an organization and is closely linked to value. Even though the importance of such specialized knowledge has waned significantly over the past few years—mainly due to the advent of advanced data-driven systems, such as those powered by AI—there are still some organizations that have domain knowledge as a requirement, particularly data-driven companies. For example, those with a biology background would most likely derive the most interesting insights and predictions related to the recently-released Covid-19 datasets.

At the very least, knowing a few things about the domain of the organization enables better communication and a more in-depth perception of the problems at hand. Even though the one-size-fits-all approach to data analytics may indeed be valuable for some cases, knowledge of how an organization is doing can go a long way and is an invaluable component of the business aspect of data science.

What's more, unlike the scientific world where things are more clear-cut and well-defined, the business world is often plagued with vague situations and ill-defined problems, oftentimes inherent in the industries these organizations operate within. Since all of these uncertainties can be alleviated through the use of data science, this gap needs to be bridged in order for a fruitful synergy to become possible. Otherwise, a lot is lost in translation and the data scientists end up solving different problems than those needing to be solved.

Getting a firm handle on this gap is essentially something a CIO or a CTO would be concerned with, though everyone involved in this has to do her part to help bridge the gap. A solid understanding of the business side of data science can be a useful aid in this.

With AI coming to the forefront of all this lately, more and more people are requesting an 'AI solution' to a problem that could be easily and thoroughly solved using a more traditional approach. Understandably, the role of statistics is also often exaggerated, yet the more knowledgeable data scientists are bound to be able to offer better solutions using conventional machine learning techniques, or custom systems combining the strengths of different models known as *ensembles*.

Finally, the matter of interpretability or transparency usually comes up when data science is summoned to provide a solution to a business problem. For the person in charge of the project, it is often the case that they want to be able to understand what's happening within a solution, instead of accepting the output on faith.

A classic example is feature importance for a predictive analytics model. Few models in data science can provide that, but it is often the case that the person in charge of the project requires this information. Of course, in other cases, a good raw performance in the form of more accurate predictions is preferable. Distinguishing, however, between these scenarios is something that is not straightforward and can baffle both the data scientist and other stakeholders of the project.

Having a good understanding of the requirements of the project, especially when it comes to things like transparency, is something that can be handled smoothly with the right level of understanding of the business side of data science and how it relates to the more nitty-gritty aspects of data science work.

Data scientist progression

In the book *Data Scientist: the Definite Guide to Becoming a Data Scientist*, the various flavors of data scientists are described, including a standard progression among some of these roles. Let's look at the latter in more detail.

For starters, there is the jack-of-all-trades data scientist, who in the beginning may be a master-of-none kind of professional. This person knows a bit of everything but is still in search of a place in the field. Such a professional is ideal for start-ups and entry-level positions in data science, though she may not be able to offer substantial expertise. However, she balances that with increased flexibility and adaptability, qualities that are invaluable to a data science team and an organization in general.

This kind of data scientist generally goes on to specialize in one of the four main kinds of data scientist: the data researcher, the data engineer, the data creative, or the data businessperson. This seemingly arbitrary classification of data scientists stems from a research text from a few years back, summarizing the view of the field at the time, in an attempt to make sense of the increasing diversity of the roles in it. Since then, however, this taxonomy has been revised as in the case of this article from Data Science Central: http://bit.ly/328UosQ.

According to this classification, the data researcher is mostly an academic data scientist with expertise in math and especially statistics, machine learning algorithms, and other high-level know-how. Naturally, people who are specializing in AI also fall into this category. Many research data scientists are also adept in scientific research, since they tend to have a PhD and a number of publications under their belts.

As for the data engineer, that's the data scientist specializing mostly in programming, and great for handling all technical aspects of the work. This data science professional is also adept in computer clusters, cloud computing, and shell scripting, while she is also knowledgeable in databases. For a larger organization this role is essential, making data engineering a self-sufficient sub-field in the data science role.

The data creative is a term for the data scientist who is more of a problem-solver and problem modeler than anything else. This person is often good in communicating information to and from the project stakeholders, putting the project requirements into a form that can be solvable through data science techniques, and figuring out how to best solve the problems at hand.

Then there is the data businessperson. This kind of data scientist is mostly geared toward handling the business aspect of the craft, mainly through leadership roles. She rarely spends time coding, though she is quite familiar with coding among other aspects of the craft. Her key strength is putting things into perspective and in managing data science projects end-to-end, while also keeping an eye on KPIs, effectively bridging the gap between the technical and business sides of the field.

Beyond all these, there is also the data versatilist, a rare role that's also very important, even if it's not mentioned in the majority of data science resources, including the aforementioned research text. This is the data scientist who is an expert in one particular aspect of the craft, but also good enough in the other aspects too, so that she can take the place of someone else if needed. This is mainly a team leader in a data science team, though she is more hands-on than the data businessperson, in many ways, and prefers to work the data over participating in business meetings.

As a data scientist gathers more experience and expertise, she generally progresses from the first role mentioned here towards the last two roles. Of course, she doesn't have to undertake every role, since there is usually some sort of specialization, especially when working in a larger organization as part of a data science team.

Data scientist skills

As a data scientist develops professionally, she acquires certain skills that enable her to progress through the aforementioned roles. Namely, a data scientist should ideally have the following skills and qualities:

Hard skills

1. **Programming in a data science language**.
   Although low-level programming can still be useful for data engineering work, languages like Julia, Python, Scala, and R are the most commonly used, with the first two having the most to offer at the time of writing.

2. **Understanding of the scientific method**. Being able to organize and conduct experiments and simulations, set up and test hypotheses, and finally analyze and present results.

3. **Mathematics**. A good handle on math, especially linear algebra and stats, is key for data science work. This includes more niche topics, such as graph theory.

4. **Machine learning**. Being able to use ML models across different methodologies is even more important than advanced stats know-how these days.

5. **Specialized skills, such as AI and NLP**. Having a good handle on modern technologies suitable for the organization is necessary, especially when an abundance of data is available to work with.

6. **Data visualization**. Creating and using visuals to demonstrate results is key for a well-done data science project.

Soft skills

1. **Communication**. Being able to understand what is expected in a data science project, communicate effectively with other professionals, and present findings to management.

2. **Problem-solving**. Since very few projects evolve as initially planned, and technical issues inevitably arise during the project, being able to problem-

solve and come up with solutions to complex situations is essential.

3. **Creativity**. Some solutions require out-of-the-box thinking. This is a very important aspect of the data science mindset overall as it enables the data scientist to tackle complex and/or novel problems.

4. **Researching new topics**. This mindset also applies to the research of new topics, since it's unlikely that a data scientist is familiar with everything in the field. Also, as new know-how comes about constantly, this skill enables the data scientist to remain up-to-date.

5. **Report writing**. Being able to put together one's findings in a comprehensive and comprehensible report is necessary, particularly if there is to be a continuation of this project.

6. **Business acumen**. The ability to understand how a business works, navigate through various policies and regulations, work harmoniously with other professionals including those in different fields, and to have a mutual understanding with management.

We'll explore in detail the key qualities of a business-savvy data scientist, particularly those related to the latter skill, in a later part of this book. Whatever the case, the more of these qualities a data scientist has, and the more developed these qualities are, the better the chances of that professional progressing to more advanced roles in data science.

Overview

The rest of the book is organized as follows. In this first part of the book, we'll look at an overview of the field, so that we are all on the same page when it comes to data science and the various technologies related to it.

In Chapter 2, we'll explain and contrast data science with AI. In Chapter 3, we'll explore how AI fits into the whole picture, and how data science currently makes use of AI techniques.

In the second part of this book, we'll discuss how data science adds value to an organization. Specifically, we'll look at business questions and data science questions (Chapter 4), the key qualities of a business-savvy data science or AI professional (Chapter 5), and the way data science helps transform the business as well as the data scientists' role in this transformation (Chapter 6).

The third part of this book is dedicated to interacting with data science professionals, something particularly useful for managers and team leaders. In the chapters that comprise this part, we'll look at the hiring process of data scientists (Chapter 7), managing a data science project (Chapter 8), and evaluating data scientists and the outcomes of data science projects (Chapter 9).

The bigger picture of this whole topic will be demonstrated in the fourth part of the book. In order to make all this content more hands-on, we've interviewed a few people involved in data science, be it as practitioners, business people, or recruiters. The highlights of these interviews will be summarized in Chapter 10, with educational resources for data science and AI practitioners provided in Chapter 11. A general summary of the book is given in Chapter 12.

We'll close the book with an appendix where complementary interview material will be made available. We'll conclude with a glossary of key terms used in this book.

Benefits

If you were to read this book in its entirety, or at least most of it, you will be able to better grasp the business side of data science and have a better handle on data-related projects. Particularly when it comes to understanding how business and data science processes interact and how business questions are answered through data analytics.

If you are an existing or aspiring manager, you'll be able to understand your data scientists better and get the most value out of their work, all while ensuring that they are a good fit in your department and your organization. This can translate into a better ROI for your investment in a data science project, a better brand for your organization, and, most importantly, better products or services that are powered by a data-driven approach rather than unreliable guesses.

If you are a hands-on data scientist, you'll explore a different yet equally interesting aspect of the craft, gaining knowledge to distinguish you from other practitioners. You'll have a better perspective when it comes to what you do in your Jupyter notebook, or whatever IDE you are using for your data science work, and how it all fits in the bigger picture. You'll graduate from being a good technical professional and gradually become an active member of a business team, interacting with other stakeholders of a project without needing an interpreter, and being seen as the wizard with the fancy science know-how!

Whatever the case, it's important to try to put all this knowledge into practice, in order to adapt it to the needs of your work and of your data science team, regardless of your role. After all, just like other data science know-how, the information in this book is as useful as you make it.

So, without any further ado, let's get started!

CHAPTER 2

Data Science and AI

About data science

Data science is an interdisciplinary field involving the methodical processing of data, particularly big data, to yield insights and build data products. Naturally, there are other potential outcomes, such as an evaluation of existing business strategies including marketing campaign efficacy, or the efficient monitoring of certain processes such as website changes. However, these can be binned into one of the aforementioned categories: insights and data products.

Data science insights and data products

Insights in data science are pieces of information that aren't obvious and usually require an in-depth processing of the data to come about. Insights are usually represented in graphics and can be leveraged to augment existing business strategies, processes, or products, or even trigger the creation of new ones—especially new features of existing products.

Since some insights are easier to obtain than others, the former usually take priority. If for example you can get a glimpse of what a good customer is like through a simple exploratory analysis, you may want to focus on that first, since the prediction of the revenue of next year's product line, for example, is bound to require more work!

The product of a rigorous analysis of data at hand which adds value to the user of your platform, is referred to as a data product. Naturally, more work is needed for the development of data products than even the more challenging insights, since a data product often involves the design of an interface, some additional engineering processes, and QA work, before it can be deployed and ready to use. Also, a data product requires maintenance, with the associated inevitable costs. Data products can be a very useful feature on a company website, a way to better understand customers, and even a catalyst for the reporting of certain processes, which would otherwise require the usage of a data scientist's time. This involves reporting the outputs of predictive models as well as any ETL processes, all of which can be automated to a great extent.

Data science pipeline

But how do these insights and data products come about? Well, it is all made possible through what is known as the data science pipeline, or data science process. In Fig. 1, the most important stages are highlighted as well as how they relate to each other.

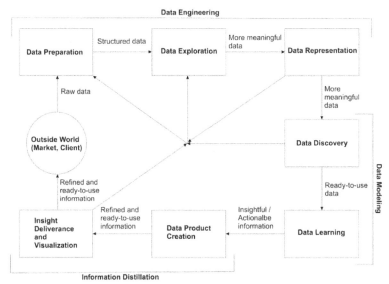

Figure 1. One representation of the data science pipeline

We start with the outside world where we get the data we are going to work with. This data usually lives in some kind of database, but it is possible that we have to acquire it from the web via an Application Programming Interface (API) or even via scraping. The data we collect is referred to as raw data and it's something we need to process before we can use it in a model. All this processing takes place in the data engineering phase.

The first step of the data engineering phase is data preparation. Here we clean up and normalize the data. We also address missing values. After these activities, we have structured data that is referred to as a dataset and is usually in the form of a data frame or a matrix.

In the next stage, data exploration, we look at various relationships among the variables of the dataset, while we also create some plots to explore the data further. It's not uncommon to use a methodology known as clustering to explore groupings too via specialized methods at this stage.

Afterwards, we proceed to data representation, a stage where the data is filtered and coded into the best-suited variables. Here we may also perform dimensionality reduction, a process that makes the dataset smaller but denser in terms of information in the variables. Much like summarizing a movie plot in a paragraph or two, we can summarize the information a dataset contains using fewer variable or combinations of the original variables.

This more meaningful data is then used in the next phase, data modeling, which consists of data discovery and data learning.

In data discovery, we explore how our data enables us to produce a useful result, such as a prediction of a particular variable—for example, a KPI.

After data discovery we have even more refined data which we can use in a model. This takes place in the data learning stage where we come up with various models for producing something of value, usually a prediction. After we have decided on a single model to use, a process that involves several testing runs, and we are ready to proceed to the final phase of the process, one that we refer to as information distillation.

At this point we are dealing with not just data but also information derived from the data. To make the most of this information we often build a data product in the first stage of this phase. The data product can be a dashboard or some API, for example, geared towards making this model we've built more widely applicable. Note that this is not always essential though, since some data science projects don't involve a data product. Whatever the case, the outcomes of the models we've built are often shared with the business people involved in the project in the next stage, namely, insight deliverance and visualization.

In this final stage, we also create a few plots, not just of the data but also of the model's performance. All this information sums up what we've accomplished in the project and distills our findings in a comprehensive form, usually a report or a presentation.

After all this, we can proceed to do additional iterations of the process, using the feedback we obtain from the outside world, and possibly some additional data. Note that throughout the process, we may go back to previous steps to refine our data and/or the models we've developed.

What data science is not

In order to better understand data science, it's useful to contrast it with what data science is not. For example, data science is not a magic box that contains all the answers and insights needed. It greatly depends on the data available, and without sufficient good quality data, it is very difficult, if not impossible, to obtain useful answers. Data science may be able to provide some useful insights, but it is unlikely to decide for you what option to pursue or solve all of the challenging problems a modern organization faces. In addition, contrary to popular belief, data science is not statistics with a bit of programming. It involves statistics, as well as other kinds of mathematics, but it has so much more when it comes to methodologies for analyzing data. Machine learning, for example, is an important component of data science, especially nowadays, while AI-based models are becoming the norm when it comes to crunching numbers. As for the more programmatic aspect of the field, it involves programming, databases, and depending on the specialization of the data scientist, some other niche know-how, such as cluster or cloud computing. Beyond that, there is also data visualization as we saw briefly previously.

What's more, data science is not something static that once you learn you are ready to apply. It requires constant education and practice as it's a highly dynamic field, much like cybersecurity. Also, academic data science books that aim to provide a complete coverage of the field are quickly outdated, as what was relevant and useful at the time those books were written may already be redundant. That's why *the data science mindset* is what is the most important, something that's always relevant and unfortunately covered in very few books.

Data science projects

Data science projects generally include various scenarios where the analysis of complex datasets is required. A classic example is the analysis of demographic data to find patterns and relationships among different attributes of the people of a country or the world at large. Particularly when you combine different datasets of this kind with other datasets, correlations can be analyzed and to some extent be predicted based on something easily measurable like income level or family size with something fairly intangible like happiness or chance of paying off a loan.

Gene expression data has become an enormous asset in biology ever since the know-how of analyzing the genome came about. However, such data is quite complex, so it's usually up to data science professionals to make sense of it. The sub-field of computational biology was born through this application of data science and is one of the most promising research-based professions these days.

The analysis of weather and other physical phenomena has started to rely more and more on data science as the amounts of data available has grown significantly and has become more diverse for conventional data analytics approaches. Many scientists today make use of data science processes to analyze the data they collect and manage it effectively.

Any Internet of Things (IoT) device generates constant data, creating a number of possibilities for insights related to the domain of the device. For example, smart watches that monitor vital signs such as pulse and oxygenation levels, along with the corresponding time stamps, enable the user of this data to draw various interesting conclusions about the person involved and even predict medical conditions in advance, all thanks to data science. Also, data products have been recently developed to assess the chances of someone being infected by Covid-19, using merely CT scan images and yielding a far better accuracy than other easy-to-deploy and scalable methods. Data science projects more geared toward business include all of the applications which can be monetized in one way or another. So, a manufacturer of an IoT system, for example, can use the data collected, analyze it with data scientists, and gain a better understanding of the customers so as to promote more relevant products to them.

Marketing has a lot to gain through data science, particularly when it comes to e-commerce. From recommendation systems like data science systems providing suggestions of relevant items to check out, to predicting the chance of success of a new product or service, to the refining of a website through A/B testing, data science has a lot to offer in this aspect of business. Moreover, the analysis of customer data to figure out relevant groupings of customers is a commonplace application of data science. Such an unsupervised learning project often expands to predictive analytics applications, whereby a new customer can be profiled in a non-discriminatory way. This relatively simple data science task can add a lot of value to an organization as discrimination can be reason for a lawsuit.

Finally, attrition prediction—if and when a client is going to stop using a company's services, particularly for companies having long-term clients—is a challenging problem that often data science is used to solve. Even though not all clients that leave do so for reasons within the company's control, it is still useful to know the chances of a client leaving and whether it would be possible to retain them through a special offer, for example.

About AI

Unlike data science, AI is geared more towards specific results of a given process and always involves optimization in some form. It can be defined as the field of computer science dealing with the emulation of human intelligence using computer systems and its application in a variety of domains. Each AI system specializes in one of the following domains.

AI as automation

AI can be viewed as a technology that enables automation on various levels. Although, it can do much more, its most direct applications involve automation of some form. The latter can be a challenging option as certain processes involve some decision-making, since not everything is as simple and straight-forward as restocking a newsstand that carries the daily newspapers.

However, for more complicated cases of restocking, involving a larger scale, AI offers some sophisticated models that take into account seasonality, variable demand due to competitors, and several other factors such as fluctuations of cost from the various suppliers. This way, the corresponding manager can focus on other, more high-level tasks, such as investigating alternative supply or warehouse options. Another example of AI automation is routing, particularly live routing as in the case of navigation systems. Such software explores various alternatives in real-time and figures out a nearly optimal option, which it conveys to the user. An absolute optimal option would take too much time and wouldn't be practical since the marginal benefit would be small. Even though this AI-based software is fairly light, in terms of computational power, it is able to handle highly complex processes, optimized for the application at hand and often leveraging the cloud. Because of its high adaptability, AI-based automation can take place in a variety of domains, even in scenarios where data science is involved, as you will see later on in this chapter.

AI algorithms

Although particular parts of AI like deep learning have become almost a synonym for AI, AI algorithms come in various shapes and forms. For instance, AI algorithms related to optimization are particularly handy, especially in cases where problems involve a lot of variables, or are highly complex in general. AI-based optimization systems are quite popular in various scenarios and there is a wide variety of applications related to them, including many other AI systems.

Computer vision is another popular field which is largely based on AI algorithms. This kind of algorithm focuses on quantifying images in a way that a computer can make sense of them and facilitate decisions related to them. For example, a computer vision system could identify potential issues in a factory's production line based on just the camera feed. Then the AI can raise an alarm and halt that production line, thereby containing the problem, until the issues are handled.

Movement-related systems have their own set of AI algorithms, such as those used in various kinds of robots, including self-driving cars. Since timing if crucial in such scenarios, these systems are built to be extra efficient and able to both understand their environment, and react, such as through a different course of action, in real-time.

Finally, applications of AI in data science have been used since the 2000s. Although these deep learning systems have been around for a while, it was only in the past few decades that they have started to be useful as computer hardware has finally caught up. We explore AI related to deep learning and optimization in more depth in our book, *AI for Data Science - Artificial Intelligence Frameworks and Functionality for Deep Learning, Optimization, and Beyond.*

What AI is not

With AI having become such a buzzword, it's easy to get carried away when talking about it and confuse the possibilities of AI with the reality of it. So, at the time of this writing, AI is not some panacea technology that can handle all sorts of problems, given the appropriate data. Other, more specialized AIs would be needed to solve these problems and someone would need to configure these AIs for the task at hand. AI that could solve problems on its own, and do so as well as a human, if not better, is what is referred to as an Artificial General Intelligence (AGI).

In addition, AI is not completely autonomous since it requires some configuration and maintenance, just like any other technology. Of course, if the problem it is asked to solve is fairly static, once the AI is configured it won't need much attention in order to function, just like the cruise-control of a car on a highway without much traffic. However, once the circumstances change, some changes will also need to take place in the AI for it to continue yielding value. Furthermore, AI is not the same as machine learning, while the latter is not a kind of AI. Machine learning involves algorithms that learn from the data using a data-driven approach instead of the model-driven approach that's usually the case for AI models. Some machine learning systems make use of AI like ANNs, but not all.

Data science versus AI

Although there are several similarities between these two fields, data science and AI differ in many ways. Data science deals with various kinds of data for the purpose of deriving insights or products, while AI aims to solve various problems, usually well-defined in a mathematical manner, in an attempt to automate or expedite the processes involved. In addition, data science involves programming and a significant amount of math, among other things, while AI makes use of certain kinds of math mostly, like calculus, and a great deal of programming. So, in a way, AI is easier to master, once you get the hang of it by learning the essentials, something that may take longer, however, than developing sufficient aptitude in data science.

Moreover, data science is more problem-focused with a methodology having applications in various domains, while AI methods are more geared towards specific applications. Nevertheless, certain AI systems, such as optimization-oriented ones, have a wider applicability than others. So, even if data science and AI work well together, they remain two distinct fields with somewhat different areas of application. Furthermore, data science is more general, covering a wide variety of methodologies, while AI is more specialized, at least for the time being. As a result, there is more room for specialization in data science than there is in AI.

Finally, data science is more closely linked to science, while AI is more like engineering. That's not to say that one is better than the other, just to highlight that a somewhat different mindset is required in each one. Still, they can effectively be combined, as we'll see soon.

The intersection between data science and AI is easy to pinpoint and important to know. Namely, it involves leveraging AI in advanced data science models, particularly for predictive analytics. This kind of model, which is entirely data-driven with no reliance on assumptions regarding data distribution, is usually in the form of special data models under the machine learning umbrella. These generally fall into two categories: network-based such as ANNs, and Fuzzy Logic-based. However, there are other AI-based systems used in data science for more specialized applications, such as certain heuristics and other niche algorithms.

Leveraging AI for data science

AI-based data science models

AI-based models in data science, such as Deep Neural Networks (DNN), are all the rage now. These are large scale ANNs, some of which are specialized for challenging tasks, such as making sense of images, natural language text, or sound clips. Also, a certain type of DNN called an *autoencoder* can compress data across fewer variables, saving both space and processing time. However, this process robs the data of its semantic meaning, so it may not be suitable for certain projects where transparency is key.

Fuzzy logic was a big step forward in AI back in the 1970s and 1980s. It involves modeling the data and the relationships among the various variables in a way that's similar to human reasoning. This new kind of logic was easy to implement and maintain, while it also offered high interpretability. AI systems based on fuzzy logic were very popular and although they don't make the headlines these days, they are still useful in data science.

AI-based data science models may be the product of other AI systems, since AI's automation capabilities have expanded there too. This is not science fiction! Nowadays there are AI systems whose whole purpose is to create and configure other AI systems, for a given task. The most rudimentary such system is the Generative Adversarial Network (GAN), which consists of two ANNs competing with each other for a predictive analytics task related to image classification, in such a way that the predictor ANN gets better and better at its job, as the other ANN tries to fool it with various images. In other words, this cunning ANN "trains" the predictor with new images somewhat similar to the images they both have seen, making the predictor better and more reliable, using a fairly limited amount of initial data.

AI-based data generation

AI-based data generation is something not many people talk about but it's a reality nowadays and something very useful in cases where there is insufficient data. It involves creating new data points based on existing data, used to train a specialized ANN. The latter is usually a variant of an autoencoder system, geared to figure out the distributions the data stems from and then generate data following the same patterns. However, a sufficiently large amount of data is required for this whole process to work satisfactorily. Alternatively, a GAN can also be used for this purpose. An AI system doesn't need the same volume of data. However, the data it can work with is usually limited to images while the images it creates are not always realistic to a human, even if they are fine as far as AI is concerned.

Tips

When delving into these fields, particularly in AI-based data science models, it's useful to keep in mind certain tips in order to make the most of these technologies. Particularly, even if data science can theoretically solve a given business problem, it requires the right data, a sufficient amount of it, and the right people to process the data. Otherwise, the data science project is bound to yield mediocre results. What's more, the tools used in a data science project are also important. Perhaps a new database (DB) system is in order for containing the relevant data for a project, or maybe a specialized toolkit is required. A knowledgeable data scientist may be able to find ways around these limitations, but it would take her more time, time that she could spend tackling the problem at hand. Besides, if it's a larger operation, perhaps it would be best to consider having a data science team or allocate some consultants or specialists to help out, at least in the beginning, before a data scientist starts working on the project.

Naturally, for AI-related data science projects, additional considerations are needed. When it comes to AI, it's important to remember that AI evolves very rapidly, making the memorization of certain methods largely insufficient as a qualification. A more dynamic and versatile approach to the field is bound to be more useful and a truly transferable skill for a candidate wishing to focus on AI professionally. What's more, just because an AI approach is intriguing, it doesn't mean that it's always suitable. It's best to try out simpler models first and if they don't yield a satisfactory performance, explore AI-based options. Besides, good data engineering can go a long way and can sometimes render conventional models adequate.

Finally, if you plan to use AI in a data science project, ensure that the person handling that implementation is knowledgeable enough in both fields. AI specialist may be great, but not what a company needs for a given data science project. Ideally, the AI know-how would be something a data scientist learns after delving into data science, since the underlying data science mindset is essential.

Key points

- Data science is an interdisciplinary field involving the methodical processing of data to yield insights and build data products.

- The data science pipeline contains seven interconnected stages: data preparation, data exploration, data representation, data discovery, data modeling, data product creation, and insight deliverance and visualization.

- AI is the field of computer science dealing with the emulation of human intelligence using computer systems and its application in a variety of domains.

- Automation is something AI is leveraged in, as in the case of product restocking, routing problems, and various other cases, across different domains.

- Data science is geared more toward specific problems while AI focuses more on specific applications, data science deals with deriving insights based on the models while AI works with problems to automate or expedite a process, and data science involves various fields including programming, while AI is geared more heavily toward programming and certain kinds of math.

- The intersection of data science and AI lies in some advanced models, usually geared towards predictive analytics. These are under the machine learning umbrella and are data-driven, while they tend to require lots of data.

- Particularly when it comes to AI, it's important to keep in mind that AI evolves very rapidly, AI-based models are not always the best way to go, and AI expertise in a professional needs to be aligned with the data science mindset for it to be most cost-effective and fruitful.

CHAPTER 3

Where AI Fits

As we discussed in the previous chapter, many people get confused about artificial intelligence and data science, and hence they use these two terms interchangeably. Even though both areas benefit from each other extensively, they have their own methods and tools. To help clarify this further, in this chapter, we provide a brief discussion of how data science makes use of AI techniques.

The most important intersection between data science and artificial intelligence is machine learning. Both fields make use of machine learning techniques quite intensively. In the case of AI, the most prominent example of how AI uses machine learning techniques is the deep learning applications that dominated the field during the last decade.

Actually, the hype around AI during these days comes mainly from the advancements in deep learning which itself is a subfield of machine learning. This is why many people confuse AI with deep learning.[1] Although the recent deep learning achievements are astonishing, the basic idea of neural networks is not new and dates back to the 1950s. That being said, with the advances in computing power and abundance of data, neural networks have become the workhorse of AI systems during the last decade.

When it comes to data science, we note that it also makes use of machine learning techniques. In this aspect, it shares some methods and algorithms that are originally coming from AI. Moreover, automation capabilities of modern AI systems are often utilized in data science.

The so called word embeddings are a great example of how data science makes use of AI-originated techniques. Word embeddings produce greater results in many natural language processing tasks than the previous approaches. In data science, we usually resort to word embeddings when working with text data. If you want to read more on the AI methods and approaches that are often used in data science, we refer you to our book, *AI for Data Science.*

Fig. 2 below demonstrates the relationship between data science, machine learning, deep learning, and artificial

---

[1] Using the words of Yoshua Bengio, one of the pioneers of the field, we can define deep learning as follows: "Deep learning is inspired by neural networks of the brain to build learning machines which discover rich and useful internal representations, computed as a composition of learned features and functions."

intelligence. Data science and artificial intelligence have many things in common but essentially, they represent two different disciplines. They both use machine learning heavily and AI is reliant on deep learning as well as other approaches like *fuzzy logic*. That being said, data science also makes use of deep learning methods.

Figure 2. The relation between data science and artificial intelligence

Before starting our discussion of what kind of methods data science borrows from artificial intelligence, we want to emphasize that deep learning methods are not the only instances of data science using AI methods. Although we restrict our attention in this chapter to deep learning, there are other methods and approaches of AI that have proven to be useful in data science like evolutionary algorithms.

The way of data science

We all live in a digital world full of data with large volumes, variety, and velocity. Veracity is also a factor to be considered, of course, constituting the fourth V of the big data phenomenon. This data can be numerical like Nasdaq stock prices or text collected from a website. The high variety in the source of data and the several different types of it necessitate the data scientists to work on every kind of data. Whether it is numerical, text, or image data, a data scientist should get the most out of them as much as possible.

Especially when it comes to text and image data, data science makes heavy use of techniques from AI. Computer vision and natural language processing tasks have been at the forefront of the AI research for quite a long time. This interest of AI research made researchers develop a comprehensive set of techniques to work with high-dimensional complex data like image, video, speech, and text. When it comes to working with this kind of data, data science relies heavily on these techniques from AI that were developed in the previous several decades. Note that in their most recent form, most of these techniques are based on deep learning methods. Let's cover two of the areas where data science makes use of AI techniques: natural language processing and computer vision.

Natural language processing

Natural language data is very common. In countless possible ways, humans produce enormous amounts of new text data every second. We send emails to our colleagues, we write comments for a product bought from an e-commerce web site, we share our ideas on Facebook, Twitter, or other social media websites. This text contains important information, as it conveys the meaning inherent in human language. It's no surprise that one of the long-standing research areas of AI is human language and the ways computers can understand human language.

The AI world has witnessed some remarkable achievements due to the deep learning revolution. Many of these achievements are from the natural language processing area, where the goal is to better understand human language. Understanding a text requires turning words into some numerical representation and this is the first place where data science borrows methods from AI.

For example, suppose that we, as data scientists, are working at a clothing company that sells its products only on e-commerce websites. We're working on a project that aims to identify whether customers like our products. We therefore collect customer reviews for our products from websites where our products are offered for sale. We process the data and end up with a dataset of customer reviews for each product in text format and their associated reviews from 1 to 5 stars. So far so good. But the methods we use in data science work on numerical data. How can we transform the text part of the reviews into something numerical?

A popular method of doing this is to use word embeddings. Word embeddings are a form of numerical representation of words. State of the art word embeddings are created by training deep learning models in an unsupervised manner. Hence, we usually use a pretrained word embedding model to turn our text data into numerical form. After this step, we can move on to the later stages of our data science project like training a supervised learning model.

Data science benefits from AI methods and hence benefits from advances in AI. This should come as no surprise as long as AI methods help data science achieve a task better than any other method.

Computer vision

Some other common use cases where data science uses AI methods arise in the field of computer vision. Computer vision seeks to understand and interpret images and videos like humans do and it's one of the oldest research areas in AI. Up until the deep learning revolution, researchers and practitioners in computer vision developed a lot of ideas and methods to tackle this hard problem. With the onset of the deep learning revolution, things have changed quite substantially in computer vision and now many state of the art methods include a form of deep learning models.

As in the point made earlier, data science makes use of AI methods especially when working with complex data like an image or a video. The central problem when tackling image data is how to create useful features that represent "good enough" information about the data. This information may include the type of objects in an image or the boundaries of certain meaningful segments. The last decade showed us that deep learning methods can be quite successful when it comes to useful representations of images.

Tips

Our treatment of the topic so far should convince you as a data scientist to learn deep learning methods. We don't mean that you should be an expert, and, indeed, deep learning has become a very broad area in itself and mastering all of its aspects doesn't make sense for many data scientists in the industry. However, being familiar with the basic methods and the ones that have proven to be useful in certain application areas like natural language processing and computer vision, would help a data scientist to enrich her data science toolkit.

Our advice for any data scientist is that the fundamentals of deep learning are something very valuable in the technology stack of data science—some deep learning methods are already indispensable for data science projects. In this respect, learning these methods should be treated as something necessary especially for the people who tend to work with text or image data.

As a result, we want to highlight that data science and artificial intelligence are two different disciplines with their own agendas. However, data science doesn't hesitate to borrow methods and approaches from artificial intelligence when doing so makes sense.

Key points

- Data science and artificial intelligence are two different disciplines.

- Data science makes use of AI methods, especially deep learning methods, when working with complex data like text, audio, image, and video.

- Natural language processing and computer vision techniques are two of the most commonly used AI methods in data science.

- Learning "deep learning" is something beneficial for a data scientist.

CHAPTER 4

Questions

Although data science can yield a lot of useful information on its own, it's not always relevant to the business, or it may not be timely. After all, a data scientist doesn't necessarily know exactly what the business needs at any given time. That's where questions come into play.

Questions, particularly those related to the business, enable the harmonious collaboration between the data science team and the rest of the organization through the establishment of clear objectives for the data scientists to pursue. Without good questions or the right interpretation of these questions into a viable course of action, data science will not offer sufficient value to the business.

Business questions and problems

First of all, what is a business question or problem? It is essential information a business needs to fix an issue or improve a product or service. This information is not something obvious or something that can come about by just discussing it in a meeting, since it stems from an underlying problem that first needs to be fully understood, before attempting a solution through a data science process, for instance.

Perhaps the same problem is analyzed through some business intelligence method with some success, or maybe the problem is too complex to be tackled this way. If it is something that requires a methodical analysis of usually different kinds of data, or involves some prediction element, then data science is the best way to go when attempting an answer.

However, not all business questions are the same, since some of them, although relevant to data, cannot be answered through a data science project, while others are too general to concern a data scientist.

Types of business questions

As with other kinds of questions, business-related ones come in various shapes and forms. From the more general to the more specific, they range in their scope and the data they require. The ones that are more relevant to the data available are those more likely to be answered satisfactorily through a data science project. However, the work of a data scientist may contribute to other, more general questions too, even if it may not be able to answer them fully.

Most of the business questions that can be answered by data science have to do with KPIs, such as sales and various profitability metrics. It's good to focus more on these since they tend to be more relevant in data-driven initiatives and more likely to yield value in a data science setting.

Examples of questions

Here are some examples of business questions:

- Among the various customers we have, who are the most profitable ones?
- What are the key attributes of the most profitable customers?
- How can I pinpoint these customers based on their key attributes?
- Will a particular new customer be profitable, i.e. a valued customer?
- What is the expected revenue from a given customer?

What all of these questions have in common is that they are quite specific and related to data we can gather or license fairly easily. Also, the underlying assumptions are met. For example, the idea that profitable customers have a lot of things in common or the fact that the answers are measurable and accessible.

All of this enables us to tackle these questions in a methodical manner through data science. Often a business question needs to be broken down to a series of simpler questions that are then tackled through data science.

Issues with business questions

The main issue with business questions is that they can sometimes be a bit vague, so they are open to different interpretations. As a result, the data scientists tackling them may understand something different than what is meant, and solve the wrong problem. Although the latter may still yield interesting insights, the answers would not add much value to the organization as they wouldn't tackle the problem the data scientists were asked to solve.

Additionally, some business questions may not be answerable with the data available, as for example the case of identifying an unusual behavior, like in fraud detection, with just a small sample of data. The latter means that the signal the data scientists try to work with is very weak, translating to unsatisfactory performance in the models they create. After all, often the harder the question, the more data is required, while the veracity of this data is something that needs to be taken into account as well.

Finally, answering business questions with data science often yields additional questions that need to be answered first, resulting in delays. So, a simple question like, "How much does that marketing campaign impact the sales?" may not be as straight-forward to answer if this campaign takes place at different times of the year, and other factors also influence the sales during these periods, such as seasonality and competitors. So, identifying how much the campaign factor correlates with these other factors may be something that needs to be examined first, before answering the original business question.

Data science questions and tasks

Questions in data science are quite different, since they are geared more towards data and what we can do with this data. Although these questions can relate to the data scientists' organization, they can appear as irrelevant. The reason is simple: they come in different varieties and are aligned with different objectives. Also, it's usually the manager's or the chief data scientist's role to coordinate these questions with the business ones we discussed previously.

Types of data science questions

Naturally, there are different kinds of data science questions too. There are questions related to variables, others related to models (particularly model performance), and others that have to do with the best ways to tackle a problem. For example, how to best reduce the dimensionality of a dataset, or how to best depict the information available.

Questions may be more specific, such as those related to the parameters of a model, and others more general or related to the methods used. Whatever the case, some of these questions can be tackled systematically, as in the case of hypothesis testing, while others require a trial-and-error approach, making the whole process more time-consuming.

Examples of questions

Some cases of the aforementioned questions are the following:

- Is a particular variable useful to have for the variable we are trying to predict?
- Is a model robust enough to deploy?
- What are the most important features in a given model?
- What evaluation metric(s) should be used for these models?
- What values should the model's parameters have for optimum performance?

- Should PCA or an autoencoder be used for this dataset to reduce its dimensionality?
- Should this information be coded as a binary variable or a continuous one?
- Should some performance be sacrificed for a more transparent model?

Naturally, the more knowledgeable and competent the data scientist, the more questions she will be able to ask, and hopefully answer. This not only enables the data science project to yield more robust results, but also covers a broader range of possibilities, yielding a more enduring and perhaps even a more versatile system being deployed at the end of the project.

Types of data science tasks

Let's now look at the various data science tasks that are available for a data scientist to use as strategies for answering the aforementioned questions. These generally fall into one of the following four categories.

- Descriptive and exploratory data analysis
- Inferential data analysis (comparisons)
- Predictive data analysis
- Causal data analysis

Data science tasks related to the first category have to do with understanding the data and exploring the various possibilities within the data. Perhaps the data is quite complex and no single data modeling approach comes to mind as the optimal choice, while there may be low-hanging fruits (insights) that can be obtained through this analysis that can help us refine the original questions. Whatever the case, this task is often useful even if other data science tasks are more relevant. For example, if our concern is gaining a better understanding of our customers through sales data, this sort of analysis would be sufficient.

Inferential data analysis has to do with comparisons and the finding of things that are not evident through the first category of data science tasks. This kind of data analysis involves statistics primarily, with emphasis on various tests that enable comparisons of different data samples, to establish if they are sufficiently different. Such an approach can help us understand whether option A is better than B, for a given KPI, for example.

Predictive data analysis, also called *predictive analytics*, is the most common data science task and has to do with creating and using a model to make predictions about the data at hand. So, if we want to know whether a given newcomer to the business is bound to be a valued customer and therefore receives special attention, predictive data analysis is the desired approach. Also, attrition (churn) detection is an application related to the same methodology.

Causal data analysis is the most challenging data science task and the one that takes the longest. Sometimes, it may not even be possible, due to the immense complexity of the problem. It involves figuring out if A causes B with a certain level of certainty. A and B may be correlated, something fairly easy to establish, but this doesn't mean that one causes the other, since they may both happen to be due to a common cause C that precedes them.

From a business to a data science question

It is essential at one point or another to turn a business question into a data science question, so that it can be solved using the methods at a data scientist's disposal. This isn't a straight-forward task and sometimes there is no one to help validate if a business question has been expressed in appropriate terms for data science to tackle it effectively. However, the whole process can be broken down into two main tasks: finding a target variable or something measurable to analyze, and selecting a data science method to apply.

Finding a target variable

The first thing that a data scientist usually does when she initiates a data science project is find a target variable or something measurable to analyze. The target variable is the distinguishing factor of a predictive analytics problem and it is something we know to some extent, but would also like to predict for some cases. For example, if we have an idea of what a valued customer is like, based on a series of measurable attributes of the various customers we have, we may want to predict whether a new customer is a valued one or not, based on these same attributes. In this case, the variable that captures the "valued customer" attribute is the target variable.

Of course, we may not always have a target variable for the problem at hand. If, for example, we are looking at figuring out the various meaningful groups of users in our online platform, we are tackling a different problem altogether. However, the data scientist will still need something measurable to analyze, such as website traffic, demographics, and telemetry data, such as clicks and pages visited. From all that, she can figure out the most similar users based on these characteristics, who are also the most dissimilar to other groups of users.

Note that even if all the data available to us is in some crude form like nominal variables or just text data, it can still be used. As long as the objective of the data science project is clearly defined, a data scientist can produce useful results from the available data, and yield some value to the whole project.

Selecting a data science method

Based on the business question, an appropriate data science method needs to be selected, facilitating answering the question. Namely:

- If we are asked to predict something based upon arbitrary data, a classification or regression approach is the way to go. If the predictions are based on sparse data or on preferences of similar items, particularly when ratings of these items are available, we'd opt for a recommendation system approach.

- If we are asked to predict something, based on time-stamped data, we'd make use of time-series analysis. This methodology usually includes other factors too, which may or may not have time stamps attached to them.

- If we are asked to figure out patterns in the data, without having something specific to predict, a clustering approach would work best.

- If we are asked to analyze text data, particularly text created by humans, even if the data contains mistakes, use natural language processing.

- If we are asked to analyze the relationships among various entities in the data available, particularly when the latter is of high complexity, a graph analytics strategy would be best.

- If we are asked to try to understand the data and depict it in a more comprehensive manner, descriptive stats and data visualization approaches would be more appropriate.

- If we are asked to compare how a KPI has changed due to some new campaign launched, or some other singular factor being applied, then an A/B testing strategy would be sufficient.

- If we need to analyze data that is complex or of a very large size, a deep learning method would be the best way to go, especially if that data involves images or sounds.

- If we need to find the best values for the parameters of a system or a problem in general, so as to maximize or minimize a given KPI, an optimization method would do the trick. If the problem is quite complex, an AI-based optimization approach would be best.

"What If" questions and sensitivity analysis

When answering a data science question, it is important to be aware of the sensitivity of the answer to the conditions of the experiment, something directly related to "what if" questions. The latter are essential for understanding the problem in more depth, and for exploring alternatives, while at the same time determining the stability of the answers. After all, the problems solved by data science are often related to complex systems and the latter are quite sensitive to the parameters used to define their functionality, much like a marketing campaign may have varying levels of effectiveness depending on the 4 P's of Marketing (product, price, place, and promotion).

The parameter search space

When building a data science model, there are always several possibilities relevant to the data at hand. Some of them may yield better performance, while others bring about a more stable model. Whatever the case, unless it's a very simple model, chances are that there are several combinations of parameters, often too many to enumerate, making searching through them the only viable option. Fortunately, through a systematic approach to this search, we can learn a lot about the model's robustness and what makes it perform well for the data at hand.

Useful "what if" questions

The aforementioned parameters are closely linked to "what if" questions. Of course, not all "what if" questions are useful for a data science project, but some such questions can add a lot of value to it. Here are some "what if" questions that are fairly useful for a data science project in general:

- What if we had more data for class X? (oversampling)
- What if there were no outliers? (extreme values)
- What if we trained the model so that it fits the data more closely? (potentially overfitting)
- What if we used a combination of models? (ensemble option)
- What if we eliminated variables X and Y? (feature selection)
- What if we merged variables X, Y, and Z in various ways? (feature engineering)
- What if we binned the (continuous) target variable? (regression vs. classification approach)
- What if we reduced the dataset? (dimensionality reduction vs. data summarization)

The butterfly effect

The butterfly effect is a fundamental characteristic of complex systems and has to do with an escalating uncertainty that stems from a minuscule change in the initial conditions. Although many people in the field don't realize it, it is an inherent part of most data science systems, particularly the more sophisticated ones that are so popular today. That's why finding the right parameters is important for data science systems to work well and reliably.

However, how reliable and robust these systems are is something that needs to be determined through a process known as *sensitivity analysis*. Otherwise, we are basically entrusting a system that may break if the initial configuration changes or if the data changes so as to make the original configuration inadequate. Since the butterfly effect in a data science model translates into an unstable and unreliable system, something no one would want to witness, it's best to avoid allowing this to happen.

Robust answers

Robust answers to questions are possible through the use of all the aforementioned aspects of business and data science questions, as well as the effective use of "what if" questions.

Confidence intervals can be quite useful in that, which is why often when we do comparisons of different data samples, we employ statistical tests—several for highly sensitive models—such as those used in time series analysis, like the ARIMA model. All these systems provide an interval for the values of the various variables they are opting to optimize, such as the coefficients of the factors involved. This way, even if they are not accurate, you can at least know what to expect and how likely it is that the prediction is off.

Although having a 100% robust answer is a pipe dream, we can at least mitigate the risk and opt for answers that are reliable enough to be useful. That's why it is often the case that several models are created and tested thoroughly, while a back-up model is made available in case the model that's deployed fails for whatever reason.

Tips

It's important to remember that in many business matters there is no single right answer, just some more and some less viable options. This means that we need to always be open to consider alternatives in the models created, as well as in the methods employed. Besides, the circumstances change rapidly, so what's not viable today may be quite feasible tomorrow.

Also, in most cases, the answer found by a data science project has an expiration data, as the data changes over time, often making previous models irrelevant. That's why maintenance is essential in a model that's been deployed, particularly when new data becomes available, or additional data streams are considered. All this illustrates that the work of a data scientist is not only something continuous but also something that's incredibly difficult to automate.

Finally, although technical expertise is essential in building and maintaining a model, it's equally important to be able to translate the business requirements accurately and think of innovative solutions, using the various data science methods and tools as building blocks. After all, if data science was purely a technical field, the differentiation among data scientists would be far more limited and the assessment of candidates in these roles far easier. We'll talk about that in the chapters to come.

Key points

- Business questions have to do with a particular problem or the potential for an improvement of a given product or service in an organization.

- The most important issues with business questions (in data science) are vagueness, inability of the questions to be answered through data science, and additional questions stemming from the answers of the original ones.

- Turning a business question into a data science one requires some understanding of what the key objective is and a good idea of what data science can accomplish. For example, we need to figure out which variable we are trying to predict or what measurable aspects of the problem to analyze, as well as to select which data science method to apply.

- Various data science tasks can match specific business requirements. For example, if we are asked to predict something, based on time-stamped data, we'd make use of a time-series analysis.

- "What If" questions and sensitivity analysis are fundamental for determining how robust a model is, something essential if that model is going to go into production.

- "What If" questions specifically can help us understand the problem better and explore useful alternatives to the model created.

- Some useful things to consider are that in many business matters there is no single right answer, just some more and some less viable options. Also, in most cases, the answer found by a data science project has an expiration date, as the data changes over time making the previous models irrelevant.

CHAPTER 5

Key Qualities

Since hiring a data science or AI professional has an inherent money and time cost, organizations try to select a candidate that will produce valuable results and work for the organization for a long time. One of the key predictors of how likely this is to happen is the candidate's business acumen.

In general, such a data science or AI professional is an asset to the organization and cares more about her work than advancing her career. She focuses on delivering value, instead of showing off her know-how or attaining job titles she can boast about. In addition, she is someone you can rely on and trust to see a project to completion. Such a professional is someone others would normally aspire to work with, in their various projects, while it's not uncommon for this person to also be an educator for her less knowledgeable teammates.

All this is great and quite easy to picture, but not exactly something you can put on a requirements document. So, let's break it down a bit, making this image of a business-savvy candidate into something more concrete.

Standard qualities

For starters, a data science or AI professional needs to be adept at her craft in terms of technical know-how. It's not so much the experience, but what she can do with what she knows that matters. Contrary to programming, where experience is paramount as it translates to development speed, in data science and AI, having been in the field for a few years more doesn't necessarily make someone a better data scientist.

Having said that, a more experienced data scientist is bound to be more suitable for a managerial position, since the additional experience would enable her to better understand other data scientists and manage them accordingly. Also, with experience often comes humility and the understanding that the field is always evolving. This is even truer with AI, which has changed drastically over the past five years.

Adaptability is also an important trait of a data scientist or AI professional. With circumstances often changing swiftly, being able to adapt is crucial. Even in universities nowadays, traditional routine-based methods are becoming increasingly rare, mainly due to the increased competition for the fairly limited grants made available for research projects. In the industry, this issue is even more pronounced since the resources are generally scarcer, while the competition landscape more variable. This uncertainty finds its way to the data science projects themselves, which are required to be more agile and easily changeable, something that makes adaptability a key quality for all the data scientists involved.

What's more, modeling a problem as a data science one is also very much valued in our craft. After all, unlike in Kaggle competitions, in the real world no data scientist is handed a readymade dataset to process and use in a predefined manner. Chances are that the data scientist not only has to assemble the dataset herself, but also figure out what kind of model she is going to use, something that she should be able to do without any guidance. This quality is hard to gauge but essential if the data scientist is to add value to the organization.

Last but not least, communication skills are crucial for data science. Even though the importance of good communication is rarely stressed in a data science or AI course, especially a boot camp, it is the one thing that can ensure smoother collaboration and a better mutual understanding between the data scientist and project stakeholders.

Communication involves both being able to listen, discern and understand what's been asked, as well as articulating and helping others to understand the relevant information of the project. It includes presentations but also meetings, email exchanges, and collaboration platforms like Slack.

Emerging qualities

In addition to the previous traditional qualities, there are also emerging qualities that are important for data science and AI professionals today. For example, flexibility is key in our ever-changing world. This quality is different than adaptability, as adaptability involves different aspects of data science work and the ability to amend existing data science methods, customizing them to the problem at hand. On the other hand, flexibility involves making compromises and figuring out ways to accomplish a task that would be impossible with a rigid approach. Naturally, both of these qualities are very useful in the data scientist role.

In addition, mentoring is something increasingly necessary nowadays, particularly when building a data science team. This is a very useful quality that involves helping other people pick up the craft. It is not the same as tutoring or teaching, though a mentor sometimes may explain something in a similar way to an instructor. Mentoring is more hands-on and is usually offered for professionals who want to improve themselves in the craft. Team leads are often required to mentor their subordinates in order to help them advance and to build rapport, thereby ensuring better performance for the team overall.

What's more, the ability to conduct research is key nowadays as the landscape of data science is rapidly changing, particularly wherever AI is involved. This is not the same as academic research which is far more demanding as a process. Research in an applied data science setting has more to do with literature reviews and an in-depth understanding of the methods or methodologies the data scientist intends on using. Especially in more advanced systems, where new developments come about constantly, research can add a lot of value and ensure an edge in performance. Research also enables the data scientist to remain relevant as a professional and advance her technical skills.

Finally, networking is also key when it comes to emerging qualities for data science and AI professionals. Although networking is useful mainly for an individual, it can also help the individual's organization. Through networking, for example, many people find new clients and partnerships. What's more, this skill can also help with recruiting new data scientists or AI experts in an organization.

Networking has never been easier, partly due to the increased number of self-organized communities through the web. It's no coincidence that many organizations have a budget for conferences, where their members go both to learn the latest trends but also to network with other professionals in their field.

Additional qualities

Apart from all these skills, there are also qualities like problem-solving abilities, creativity, time management, and report writing that factor in when it comes to applying data science or AI in an organization.

Problem-solving involves taking up a challenge and finding a viable solution, even when a problem seems daunting at first. The solution may not be the best, but it works well enough, something that is often preferable to a perfect solution that is impractical to implement. Problem-solving is also a good proxy of a data scientist's engineering training. It's this specialized training that differentiates her from the more math-based analytics disciplines, such as the business intelligence professional. Problem-solving is particularly useful in challenging scenarios where the way to solve a problem is unclear or complex.

Creativity is like problem-solving but goes a step further. Instead of employing conventional approaches it ventures into novel ones, sometimes borderline silly. Yet, these approaches can work and may yield better results, at least in terms of efficiency. However, creativity is not as simple as it is portrayed in the arts world, since in science it is based on the mastery of the conventional methods and a sharp sense of discernment.

Time management is primarily about keeping to a schedule and meeting deadlines. It's an essential organizational skill that many data scientists struggle with. After all, it's often difficult to assess how much time a certain task would take since data science is not a clear-cut process, even if its stages are well-defined.

The data may be problematic or insufficient, or the model built may perform inadequately. Whatever the case, it takes certain skill to be able to predict what issues may arise in a data science project and budget sufficient time to tackle them, all the while disciplining yourself to stay on track even when more interesting options come about as you analyze the data.

Report writing in data science involves creating comprehensive yet succinct reports describing a data science project. A good report is much more than structured and formatted notes. It has to do with linking the results of the experiments with the corresponding questions. After all, a report is for the stakeholders of the projects, particularly management, so it has to keep jargon to a minimum and put a lot of emphasis on deliverables and how the data science work fits into the bigger picture, all while using comprehensive graphics to illustrate the key points of the project.

Tackling a business problem

When you have a business problem to solve and the preliminary analysis of it shows that it needs to be handled using a more advanced analytics approach, such as data science, with or without AI, then you need someone who can deliver something reliably. Fortunately, there are business-savvy data science professionals who can accomplish that, even though for a newcomer to the field it may seem like a daunting task. So let's discuss how a business-savvy data science or AI professional would solve a business problem.

First of all, before taking any action whatsoever, a business-savvy data scientist would listen to the stakeholders and note down anything that can be used as a requirement or specification for the project. The focus would be to try to get as much information as possible and couple it with her domain knowledge. Also, a survey of the available data would be made, as well as considerations regarding what other data streams can augment the original dataset.

Then she would attempt to pair the information gathered with one or more of the methodologies relevant to the business questions. She would discuss the methodologies with any external consultants, gaining a better perspective, exploring new possibilities, and taking into account other relevant data science-related information.

Then, the business-savvy data scientist or AI professional would begin implementing a Proof-of-Concept (PoC) solution which would attempt to solve at least part of the problem. This shouldn't take very long and the amount of data used is bound to be limited. Once the PoC is finished, it would be discussed with other project stakeholders to examine if it is designed to solve the original business problem.

Upon completion of the PoC, she would implement a more in-depth solution, making use of additional data and computational resources. Some clear deliverables would be agreed before starting this part of the solution, so as to manage everyone's expectations satisfactorily. Once the project is finished, she would present it to the project stakeholders, along with ideas about how it can be changed if necessary and how an additional iteration of the data science process might improve the results, particularly if additional data was to be gathered.

Of course, throughout this process, regular updates and meetings would be held with project stakeholders, beyond just the final presentation. Depending on the project, an Agile management approach might be employed, instead of the traditional waterfall model. Finally, some research on various options for each stage of the pipeline would be conducted, either by the data scientist in charge of the project, or by one of the members of her team, to ensure an optimal approach.

Tips

Beyond all that, it's important to consider certain traits that are more difficult to define. For example, a candidate's personality and eagerness to evolve as a professional, something often referred to as ambition, may be an important factor since a professional like this is bound to make a bigger effort to work well with her peers.

What's more, a candidate's natural curiosity, which usually translates to a willingness to learn and evolve her aptitude in the craft, is noteworthy. Unfortunately, both of these personality traits are next to impossible to include as bullet points in a resume or mention them in a cover letter without appearing pretentious.

In addition, a candidate's approach to technology and to the data science field in general is crucial, although that too is very difficult to put into words. Nowadays there are some tech people, particularly in the field of AI, who tend to see new tech as something borderline mystical. This is no exaggeration, mind you, considering that many advocates of this approach have decided to view AI as a deity rather than as a useful asset that is here to facilitate our lives. A data science or AI professional with her feet on the ground would be generally preferable for an organization that cares more about results than sci-fi concepts.

What's more, a candidate's ability to work well with others is something essential, particularly in organizations having a data science team. After all, the era of silos is over and, now more than ever before, workers are required to work in unison. This is partly due to the complexity of the problems tackled these days. However, collaboration also makes for better work relationships and increased performance, particularly in cases where a large spectrum of skills is required to tackle a problem. As you probably know, data science and AI related problems fall into this category, making collaboration among the corresponding professionals essential.

Finally, a candidate's sense of loyalty to the craft is particularly important, especially in this world of constantly emerging entertainment-related technologies, such as virtual and augmented reality, that may make data science appear less intriguing for those more prone to thrill-seeking behavior. This is something that has been observed in many software engineering jobs, where competent programmers decided to shift to other fields like AI. It's not far-fetched for data scientists or AI professionals to do the same, particularly if they are not inherently intrigued by these fields.

Some of us would do data science even if we were the last people on the planet. This is due to an intrinsic fascination with the craft. Harnessing this quality would lead to a long and mutually beneficial working relationship between data science practitioners and employers who are able to value this quality. After all, it's qualities like this one that make up your individuality as a data science professional, helping you stand out from the crowd as a valuable resource for an organization.

Key points

- There are various standard qualities data science and AI professionals should ideally have, such as technical aptitude and know-how, adaptability, and modeling and communication skills.

- There are also some emerging qualities that are becoming more relevant to today's world, such as flexibility, mentoring ability, research, and networking.

- There are several other qualities to consider, such as problem-solving ability, creativity, time management, and report writing.

- There are also some useful considerations to have when evaluating a data science or AI candidate, such as personality and ambition, approach to technology, collaboration ability, and loyalty to the craft.

CHAPTER 6

How Data Science
Transforms Business

"A data scientist is someone who can look like a business person to the technical people and a technical person to the business people at the same time."

We're all living in a digital world where things change quite rapidly. This is also true for businesses, as new ideas can find their way quite swiftly to disrupt established corporations that were with us for centuries. That's why everybody talks about the digital transformation, and that's why everybody emphasizes the effective use of the data against the harsh competitions of the 21st century.

Data scientists with a proper business acumen lie at the center of any successful digital transformation. In this chapter, we'll cover how data science transforms businesses around the world and how a data scientist can acquire the business knowledge needed to contribute to the resilient future of a company. This is not to claim that data scientists are the only actors in a digital transformation, but rather a tribute to the importance of data science and its interaction with the business.

Data science impact

Even in centuries-old industries, we see substantial changes that occur with the help of data. Data-driven transformation touches almost every aspect of how industries like retail, automotive, and finance operate. These industries have long histories, but still, they are all undergoing substantial transformations with the help of data science. We classify data-driven transformations into two types:

1. Factors that affect business outcomes with the help of data. An important benefit of data science for business is that one can derive causal relationships that are critical for the success of operations and strategies. As an example, consider how financial institutions approach credit-scoring. Beyond traditional approaches, almost all financial institutions nowadays score the creditworthiness of a customer using machine learning models. These models estimate factors like age, income, among others, on the creditworthiness of a customer using historical data with unparalleled efficiency.

2. Automation. Many processes and services that were done manually or using rule-based methods can now be automated with the help of data science. Advances in AI in the last decade make AI systems capable of solving critical tasks in

computer vision and natural language processing at a level even better than that of an average human. This so called "deep learning revolution" has fostered a strong transformational wave in several industries. As an example, think about autonomous driving. Even though there's still some time before achieving fully autonomous driving, assistant pilot technologies in cars already offer quite advanced capabilities.

Irrespective of whether we're talking about deriving insights from data or automating a process, we want to highlight the role of a business-savvy data scientist. A data scientist with good domain knowledge in finance can contribute in many ways to the future of a financial institution. Similarly, a data scientist with experience in the automotive sector can leverage the power of data to transform her company.

Reflections on a centuries-old industry

The history of financial institutions goes back to medieval times. As one of the oldest industries, finance has preserved its special position in the world economy. In a nutshell, based on lending and providing liquidity, the finance industry has clearly understood the importance of data and is one of the industries that employs many data scientists. To give a sense of how data science changed this industry in recent years, we want to outline some areas in finance where data science plays a central role:

- **Better risk assessment**: All lending activities that occur in banks rely on the risk assessment and the creditworthiness of the customers. Data scientists build machine learning models to measure the risk level involved in a lending transaction. We can confidently state that in almost all major banks, risk assessments and credit-scoring are done using data science techniques. Hence, data scientists stay at the heart of the most fundamental operations of the finance industry.

- **Better fraud detection**: Detecting and preventing fraud is something very important both for financial intermediaries as well as legal institutions. With advances in data science, fraud detection is done mainly using machine learning algorithms. Historically, detecting fraud in finance has been done using rule-based systems. Nowadays, the majority of financial intermediaries have transitioned from rule-based systems to machine learning systems to get better at detecting fraud.

- **Autonomous trading**: Understanding the patterns and trends behind stock or equity prices is a very complex problem. Recently, deep reinforcement learning has become quite popular in building autonomous trading systems. In 2000, there were 600 traders at the Goldman Sachs U.S. cash equities trading desk. In 2017, only two remained.[2] This figure highlights the dramatic transformation that financial trading went through in the last decade.

- **Autonomous banking**: Recent years have witnessed even more radical changes to the finance industry. So-called autonomous banking, using data science, promises swifter processes in credit lending and money transfers without the intervention of humans.

- **Customer support**: Serving millions of customers isn't a trivial thing and customer satisfaction is vital in the banking sector. Among other services, conversational AI systems in the form of chatbots are now quite common in retail banking. The technology behind conversational AI is natural language processing and advances in this field in the last decade have made it possible to interact with customers using chatbots.

The areas we outlined above are just a small sample of those that can be found in finance. Data scientists that have

---

[2] https://bit.ly/2U8NQbn.

a strong knowledge in the financial sector will no doubt play critical roles in the upcoming decades.

How to acquire domain knowledge

The use case of finance illustrated how even centuries-old industries are changing with data. As we emphasized several times, the key player in this transformation is the data scientist with strong domain knowledge. No matter what the industry is, a data scientist with strong business knowledge is one who can combine the technical capabilities of ever-evolving data science with the specific requirements of the business area.

Now that we saw how industries are changing, let's talk about how data scientists can acquire domain knowledge. As we emphasized throughout this book, augmenting technical knowledge with domain knowledge is what makes a data scientist an indispensable part of the modern business world. Here, we provide a set of suggestions that enable a data scientist to gather business knowledge. The list is not intended to be comprehensive, but we have selected points with proven effectiveness in knowledge acquisition.

- **Learning by doing:** Although some business areas can be learned in universities to some degree, real learning occurs when someone starts to work in a company. You can find abundant resources when it comes to learning the technical side of the data science. However, you'll realize that learning platforms that teach the business aspect of data science are very rare. Hence, learning the business side of a data science project occurs on the job.

- **Finding a good mentor**: Benefiting from the knowledge of others is a proven method of gaining knowledge. This is also the case when learning the business side of data science.

- **Questioning in terms of business rationale**: What we mean is that as a data scientist you need to approach your technical work as a critic of the business logic behind it. When you start to question the rationale behind the work you do, you start to get accustomed with the business processes at play.

- **Learning business jargon**: Knowing business terms, especially those circulating in meetings, not only urges you to understand those concepts but also helps when you need to communicate your findings to non-technical people.

- **Attending meetings, conferences, talks, or other events**: Ideally, a business-savvy data scientist should be someone who can attend a meeting with business units and discuss the business ideas with other non-technical people in that meeting without any difficulty. This is how a data scientist can be a bridge between the technical world of data and the business surface surrounding it. That is why we say a data scientist is someone who can look like a business person to the technical people and a technical person to the business people.

Data scientist's role in digital transformation

When we talk about the importance of communication in data science, we don't mean just the importance of conveying some technical results to the business people and management, but we also mean that data scientists' work serves as a communication channel in the company between the hard truth in the data and business strategies and operations. The impact of data science on supporting decision-making in a company cannot be overemphasized. Transforming traditional long-standing business models comes with a lot of challenges and obstacles. To overcome these, companies should first see the potential value of going through this transformation. And this value can only be seen in the light of data. From this perspective, data scientists with strong business acumen can work as facilitators and catalyzers. They conduct scientific experiments and shed light on the potential value of going through digital transformation.

Data science's role as a supporting mechanism of decision-making is not backward- but forward-looking. Shedding light on future business plans both in terms of strategic decisions and operational decisions is a key factor in understanding the benefits of going through a transformation. Hence, good data scientists work as navigators in a company when uncertainties as well as opportunities are waiting in the future. Last but not least, data scientists are those technical people who implement the data science projects. Hence, thinking about digital transformation without data scientists is not possible.

Tips

Being the hero of digital transformation requires you to invest in yourself. This investment is three-fold:

1. Invest in the technical aspect of your job. Learn new technologies, go in-depth in what you're familiar with, and experiment with new methods.

2. Invest in the business aspect of your job. Don't hesitate to attend business meetings, interact with business people, and read materials on the business background of your work.

3. Invest in your communication skills. Get yourself familiar with the business terminology, practice on

presenting technical results in clear non-technical terms. Are you afraid of public speaking? Then, go ahead and challenge yourself. Try to attend conferences and meet-ups not just as a listener but also as a speaker.

In order to transforms a business, data scientists should stay on top of the ever-changing technology field. Keep yourself up-to-date in every aspect of your job.

Key points

- Data science's impact on businesses can be categorized into data science supporting decision-making by discovering relationships in the data, and automating processes and services.

- Even centuries-old industries like finance are changing radically thanks to data science.

- Data scientists need to augment their technical capabilities with business knowledge in order to navigate their companies in the digital transformation.

- Data scientists with strong business acumen work as facilitators and catalyzers in the digital transformation of a company.

CHAPTER 7

Hiring Data Science Professionals

"It doesn't make sense to hire smart people and then tell them what to do. We hire smart people so they can tell us what to do." - *Steve Jobs: His Own Words and Wisdom*

Probably the most valuable asset a company has is its human resources, or "human capital." This is also the case when it comes to your company's data science capabilities. The most valuable assets your company can have are not hardware or the software but people, especially self-motivated team players.

Building great teams is neither easy nor cheap. It usually takes a long time to hire the right people. In this chapter, we'll walk you through the steps of hiring the right data science professionals. Although you shouldn't take the practices we'll present here as set in stone, the points we'll make are best practices established in the data science community over the last decade.

Although there are some well-known practices in hiring technical staff, hiring data scientists comes with its own peculiarities in comparison to hiring other technical people like software engineers. The main reason for this is that a data scientist is not just a technical employee but also a bridge between the technical and business side of your company. Hence, communication skills in data science are essential. Moreover, domain expertise is also something valuable in the tech stack of a data scientist. Finding talent with relevant domain expertise for your business poses another challenge in the hiring process.

When hiring data scientists, the interview process should take into consideration all the fundamental skills required of a data scientist. As covered earlier, we can summarize the skill set of a data scientist as shown in Fig. 3.

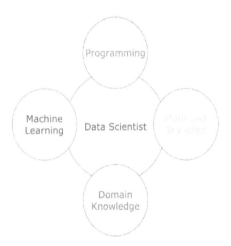

Figure 3. Fundamental skill set of a data scientist

- **Programming:** Without proper programming skills, no one can become a data scientist.

- **Math and Statistics:** These disciplines are crucial in the sense that, without their knowledge, one can't understand and explain what she is doing and why.

- **Machine Learning:** One of the critical parts of a data science project is to train good models to achieve a specific task. To this end, a data scientist should be quite familiar with the fundamentals of machine learning.

- **Domain Knowledge:** Domain knowledge is something found rarely. So, a data scientist with a proper domain knowledge is someone who is valuable for any company.

In the rest of this chapter, we'll talk about how to hire a data science professional. The important point is that a successful hiring process should help you discover the level of the candidate in these four skills.

Start with the team lead

If you're starting to form a data science team from scratch, the first step you need to take is to hire the right tech lead for this team. This person can help you hire the rest of the team. In addition, finding people with relevant domain expertise along with technical capabilities is a challenge.

Hence, hiring a tech lead with good domain knowledge and technical skills would ensure that even if you can't find other data scientists with domain knowledge, this technical lead can help them acquire those skills gradually.

Hiring a team lead means hiring someone who is experienced enough to manage a team as well as someone with great hands-on coding capabilities. Thus, this role involves a lot of responsibilities and a degree of freedom to pursue an independently determined agenda. When hiring your team lead, you need to take into account the following skills and abilities:

- **Coding**: Although it should not be considered a must, having mastery of several languages would be something useful because, when hiring the other members of the team, you can be flexible about the programming language the team will be using. For example, if the team lead has experience with both Python and Julia, you can hire flexibly from the pool of candidates with knowledge of at least one of these.

- **Statistical knowledge**: The success of a data science project usually hinges on whether the team members have enough of this skill at their disposal.

- **Domain knowledge**: Ideally the team lead should have previous experience in the domain your company operates within. Note that finding this kind of person is not easy. This is rather a "good to have" rather than a "must have."

- **Team management skills**: This is important for the successful implementation of projects as well as cooperation between team members. Having someone who can organize her time as well as the time of other team members is key for a promising and successful team.

The technical framework for hiring data scientists

Now, we can start discussing the best way to hire data scientists. Assessing the capabilities of someone as a data scientist is not an easy task. It requires you to assess the capabilities of a person from different perspectives in a very short period of time and with a limited number of interactions. Thus, following a framework could help you get the most out of the hiring process. Let's first discuss what kind of skills this framework can assess:

- **Coding skills:** Having a solid programming background is a must have for any data scientist. Most of the time, data scientists work on writing programs to solve some specific task whether this task is model-training or putting a model into production. In every case, a data scientist should know how to write efficient code. Moreover, being familiar with object-oriented programming principles is also something useful.

- **Data processing and data munging skills**: A majority of a data scientist's time is spent on data cleaning and data processing. Hence, a data scientist candidate should be able to swiftly write data processing code as well as being able to justify steps taken during the processing stage.

- **Machine learning skills**: Often the ultimate goal in a data science project is to predict something or get insights regarding what causes some phenomenon. Both of these goals are handled with machine learning methods. Hence, a data scientist candidate should know the fundamental methods in machine learning like ANNs and random forests as well as fundamental concepts like overfitting, regularization, and confusion matrices.

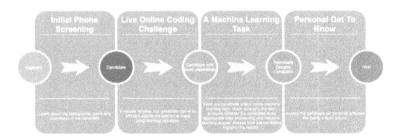

Figure 4. Four-step framework for hiring data scientist

In order to evaluate someone's capabilities in these areas, the following framework is something very useful:

1. Initial phone screening

The first step in hiring a data scientist is to understand whether an applicant seems to be a good fit for the role. We say "seems to be," because discovering a good fit requires many interactions between the applicant and the company. A good first step is to arrange a call. In this first conversation, the following areas would help to get an initial impression about the candidate's fit:

- **What kind of background**: To learn about this, you may ask the candidate to briefly talk about her previous work experiences and projects.

- **What kind of career path** the candidate is looking for in the long term: The idea is to learn whether the candidate is looking for a technical position and wants to pursue a role where they can continue to be a technical person or if they want to switch to a more business-related role. This is critical for medium- to long-term engagement between the candidate and the company.

Then, the interviewer can give some brief information about your company and what kind of projects the team is or might be working on. This summary would make the candidate more clearly understand the requirement of the position. This first phase of the hiring process could take between 15 to 30 minutes. The applicants who seem be a good fit can be invited to the next phase.

2. Live online coding challenge

After the first screening, evaluate the programming skills of the applicant. For this purpose, we recommend arranging an online coding challenge interview with the candidate. The interviewer in this phase could be someone senior from a software development team.

In this phase, the key is to evaluate whether the candidate understands the difference between an inefficient implementation of an algorithm and an efficient one. To this end, the interviewer can ask a question that can be implemented easily. However, the easiest possible implementation should be something that has a high order of time complexity. If the interviewee implements a solution that is suboptimal, then the interviewer can walk through with her to implement a more efficient one. During this, the interviewer should observe whether the candidate can understand the guidance clearly and improve the time complexity of her implementation.

Successful candidates in this phase are those who can directly write efficient codes or those who can improve the time complexity of their implementations. Don't expect that a person should come up with the best solution on the first attempt. The next step in this same interview is to ask the candidate questions about some basic principles of programming or some basic data structures. The questions may cover object-oriented programming concepts as well.

3. A machine learning task

Probably the most important step in the hiring process of a data scientist is to understand whether the candidate is proficient in machine learning. To be able to do this, one of the best ways is to send a take-home task to the candidate and ask them to return it back within one week. The take-home task can involve preparing an anonymized sample of your company's data. Send the data with a set of general-purpose requests to the candidate. The tasks below can then be requested:

- Clean the data and perform preprocessing.

- Do some feature engineering to come up with a set of useful features for the subsequent machine learning models.

- Implement a couple of machine learning models that are suitable for solving the task at hand. Select the best model and explain why it was selected.

- Discuss the results. In doing so, make sure that the readers of this result part are composed of people both from a technical background as well as a non-technical background. The candidate should be able to explain findings in layman's terms.

Once you get back the results from the candidate, investigate the responses and evaluate whether the candidate is successful on the following points:

- They can process data. The data cleaning steps are relevant and the preprocessing has been performed appropriately.

- They are competent at feature engineering. The candidate should have evaluated the importance of the features and select the best set according to some scientific criteria.

- They can implement a machine learning pipeline including splitting the data into training, test, and validation sets; performing hyperparameter selection; and evaluating the models correctly.

- The candidate is able to communicate technical findings to a non-technical audience. The purpose of this is to assess whether the candidate is capable of converting scientific and technical terms into something that can be easily understandable by people without technical knowledge.

4. Personal interview

The last stage in the interview process is to meet the candidate in person. Making face-to-face contact has its own value. Moreover, in this stage, one can also organize the interview so that the points from the previous interview stages where the candidate seems to be lacking on some topics can be discussed in more detail. This means that this last step of the hiring process could be a hybrid of personal and technical interview.

Once all the interview stages are completed, the time arrives for reaching a decision on whether to hire the candidate or not. The framework we presented in this chapter is distilled from our experiences. Thus, playing with it and augmenting it with some other useful evaluation methods can help you build a successful data science team, or prepare you for the hiring process if you are a potential candidate.

Tips

Hiring the right people is a challenge. Data science is an interdisciplinary field and hiring data scientists has its own peculiarities. Setting guiding principles and following useful frameworks would enable an organization to take the right decisions in the hiring process. In this chapter, we've proposed a four-stage framework that you can follow in building a data science team.

When interviewing data scientist candidates, the crucial point is that you should be able to evaluate the multiple facets of a data science professional. Programming, statistics, machine learning, and domain expertise are all important constituents of data science. Hence, when it comes to data science, the interview process should have multiple stages that enable you to understand the capabilities of the candidates in terms of all of the aspects of data science. Following the time-tested framework from this chapter would be useful in this regard.

Key points

- Hiring data scientists differs from hiring technical people for software engineering.

- The key skills that a data scientist should have are programming, math and statistics, machine learning, and domain knowledge.

- A four-step framework for hiring data scientists can enable you to evaluate the skill sets of data scientist candidates. These steps are initial phone screening, online coding challenge, take-home machine learning task, and personal interview.

CHAPTER 8

Managing a Data Science Project

The professional world is organized in such a way that teams consisting of several people are the basic building blocks responsible for the realization of specific tasks and projects. These teams should work in a coherent manner so that collective action would produce products and services of high quality. In this chapter, learn how to manage a team of data scientists as we cover some basic properties of a typical data science project and highlight how a data scientist can work efficiently in this environment.

Agile methods

In today's business world, the most commonly adapted project management method is known as *Agile*. As an alternative to classical Waterfall methodologies, Agile methods emphasize the ever-changing nature of project requirements even during implementation, and hence they use time frames as short as one week. These short periods are called *sprints*. There are different approaches to Agile project management such as Scrum and Kanban. Agile methodologies are the main way of planning and realizing projects in the business world, when it comes to projects with highly dynamic circumstances or feedback loops.

Data science projects are no exception in this regard, and they are also often managed using Agile methods. A good data scientist should be familiar with the basics of how a data science project can be managed under an Agile approach. That being said, data science projects have their own peculiarities and sometimes don't fit into Agile frameworks like scrum. Before moving further on the specific features of a typical data science project, let's discuss how scrum works.

Scrum framework

Being the most common Agile framework in business, scrum is the most common methodology used in data science projects. Hence, understanding scrum is key to the success of a data science team. The scrum framework was proposed by Jeff Sutherland and Ken Schwaber in the 1990s. Since its onset, it has become one of the most common project management frameworks.

Before getting started on how scrum works, let's first mention the roles scrum defines for people working on a project. These are:

- **Product owner:** sets the vision for the project or product. He's also the one that fills in the backlog as we'll discuss shortly.

- **Scrum master:** leads the project. In this sense, this role is the project manager role.

- **Developers:** team members who complete tasks.

Of these three roles, data scientists usually work as developers. They are responsible for implementing tasks and delivering the project. Once a project is initiated, the work that needs to be done should be planned to be completed in a limited time frame. The product owner lists the tasks in the backlog. The backlog is the place where the project is divided into small tasks.

Scrum works as consecutive sprints of work delivery. Sprints are the main planning and implementation units of the scrum framework. Typically, a sprint spans a week. At the beginning of a week, a new sprint starts. In the weekly planning meeting, some tasks from backlogs are transferred to the sprint board. Each task is assigned to a specific person or a small group. Then, every morning that week, a short meeting of typically 15 minutes is held to ensure that everyone works on the tasks assigned. At the end of each week, a review meeting is held to discuss how the sprint has gone and whether the tasks are realized. Unaccomplished tasks are transferred back to the backlog or to the board of the next sprint. Fig. 5 referenced from scrum.org demonstrates how the scrum methodology works through sprints.

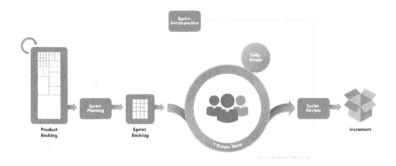

Figure 5. Graphical illustration of how Scrum works

As mentioned, sprints in the scrum methodology usually take one week. However, some machine learning models take weeks to train! How can one combine the scrum framework with the peculiarities of a data science project?

Iterative nature of a data science project

A data science project consists of several stages. Assuming that the data to be worked on is already stored somewhere, the phases of a data science project can be outlined as follows:

- Access data stored in different places, combine and store in a single place.

- Data cleaning, data preprocessing, and feature engineering steps can be quite involved in terms of work load. Moreover, the desired outcome of this phase can't be accomplished in a single shot of consecutive steps. Many iterations should take place.

- Machine learning. This phase involves many stages, including training and evaluating several machine learning models to the tuning the hyperparameters. This phase is also an iterative phase.

- Production. In this phase, the trained models are moved to a production environment where they can be deployed as (web) services.

A data science project pipeline consists of stages that exhibit an iterative nature. Organizing these iterative phases as one week-long sprints is not something trivial. Instead, a task in a single phase like data cleaning should be revisited multiple times over the life of the project. Let's give an example to demonstrate this scenario.

Especially when working with big data, discovering problematic values in the data becomes a real challenge. Say that we have an ever-growing database that is filled with the text data of customer reviews from a streaming source like a website of an e-commerce company. Each day millions of new records are added to this database.

Given the very large number of observations, how can we identify all the problematic values in our data? Even if we could somehow achieve this for a snapshot of the database, every day new kinds of unwanted values might appear in this database. So, data cleaning is not something that can be done in a single go for this scenario. Instead, the data should be investigated periodically to discover new types of problematic inputs to be cleaned. Moreover, as new problems are discovered, all of the data cleaning processes may need to be run again.

Considering this scenario, one can see why a one week scrum sprint is not the perfect way of handling this data cleaning task. Even more, a data science project is full of experiments and iterations similar to what we gave as an example.

Next, we will look at another common aspect of a typical data science project that exhibits difficulties hard to manage in scrum.

Ambiguities and unknowns

Say that you, as a data scientist, are assigned to an interesting project and asked to make an estimation of the accuracy of your final model. You don't know much about the quality of the data, you don't know how to come up with a good set of features, and you don't know a benchmark that you can compare the performance of your model against. Would coming up with a good estimate be something easy for you?

The answer of the above question depends on many unknowns and these are what we want to bring to your attention.

As we pointed out many times before, a data science project is comprised of multiple phases. Each phase is full of uncertainties that make it hard to estimate the time required to complete that phase.

For example, often the first step in a data cleaning phase is to discover problematic values in the features. Recall the data cleaning challenge that came up while discussing the iterative nature of this phase. If we're working on really big data, discovering problematic values is a real challenge which requires a lot of iterations. So, when such a task is transitioned from the backlog to a sprint board, a reasonable time estimate should also be provided. In order to estimate the time frame, one should have an answer to the following unknowns:

- What kind of problems do we anticipate in the data?
- How many times do these problematic values occur in the data?
- What are the best ways to handle these problems?

Unfortunately, in many cases these questions are hard to answer with a simple rule. Now, taking into account the iterative nature of the process, another challenge is to estimate the number of iterations that will be needed.

These unknowns are common in almost every stage of data science work. As another example, let's think about building a machine learning model. When setting a goal for the final performance of a model at the beginning of a data science project, one needs to give an estimate of accuracy, or another suitable metric. Setting a goal for the final performance of a machine learning system is especially challenging if nothing similar is publicly known as a benchmark. These unknowns and ambiguities make data science project management hard to implement in a scrum setting.

Fitting a data science project into scrum

A priority for any a successfully completed project has to be having the right team that can work in a flexible yet organized atmosphere. Data science projects are no exception. The first thing to settle when beginning a data science project is to assign people to suitable roles. In the scrum setting, there are three roles that need to be assigned.

Recall that in scrum most data scientists will work as developers. These people are the hands-on technical people who are responsible for implementation. In data science projects, a smart choice for the role of scrum master would be someone who is a seasoned data scientist with sufficient experience in managing a team. When it comes to product owner, the possibilities are broader.

We see product owners from very different backgrounds like software development or sales and marketing. If the product at hand is a data science service or product, then an ideal product owner would also be someone who is at least familiar with the basics of data science. Moreover, this person should also have sufficient knowledge about what data science can and can't do!

Now let's talk about how to create tasks that can be handled within the scrum framework. As we highlighted in this chapter, data science projects involve several iterative phases as well as many unknowns and ambiguities. Thus, a successful project management using scrum requires designing clever backlog and small tasks for the iterative processes as well as the unknowns. To this end, we provide the following guidelines:

- Create the backlog by taking into consideration the consecutive phases of a standard data science pipeline. Recall Fig. 1 and Fig. 6.

- To deal with ambiguities and unknowns, make tasks as small as possible. For example, for the data cleaning phase, don't open a task like "do data cleaning." Instead, create tasks that are more narrowly focused like "calculate the ratios of missing values in each feature."

- To deal with the possible iterations of a task, use a simple versioning method. For example, when starting data cleaning, create the task for it as "calculate the ratios of missing values in each feature". When another iteration is needed in the life cycle of the project, create the tasks for the same phase as "calculate the ratios of missing values in each feature," "calculate the ratios of missing values in each feature," etc.

- If your role in the project is scrum master, be prepared for missing deadlines for some tasks especially at the beginning of the project. For example, training a deep learning model might take longer than what you calculated. So, each time you are confronted with this kind of situation, align your expectations accordingly.

- If your role in the project is product owner, be prepared that the outcomes targeted at the beginning of the project might have to be dropped as the project progresses. Keep your expectations slightly lower than what is set at the onset of the project, especially for novel projects where new kinds of datasets and machine learning models are on the table.

Tips

To implement good projects, you need to know how to organize the tasks and the workforce around the project. Scrum framework gives us a way of doing so. Since scrum is the de-facto standard of managing projects in the IT world, the challenge is to fit data science projects into that framework effectively.

Key points

- Know the scrum framework well. The more you make yourself accustomed with it, the more you know its limitations and strengths.

- A data science project consists of several phases that are tied to each other. However, jumping back from a late stage to an earlier one is common and its due to the iterative nature of the data science work.

- Managing data science projects is different from managing software development projects. A data science project involves a lot of experimentation and a ton of iteration. Managing a data science project using the scrum framework poses some challenges that can only be resolved with a clear understanding of what the data science project lifecycle is.

- In data science projects, ambiguities and unknowns make it hard to estimate the required time for completing some tasks.

CHAPTER 9

Managing Data Scientists

In previous chapters, we've talked about how to recruit data scientists and how to manage data science projects. One additional aspect that we haven't covered so far is how we should manage data scientists and how we might evaluate their performance. This aspect is as critical as hiring the right people or managing the data science project, especially in a field that is dynamic and ever-evolving. Hence, we won't give a set of very simple and easily adoptable rules to follow in a business environment. Rather, we'll try to provide some general principles deemed beneficial from experience for managing human resources in data science teams over the last decade.

Let's start with discussing how we can evaluate outcomes in a data science project.

Evaluate a data science project

The deliverables of data science projects usually come with inherent uncertainties that make them hard to evaluate. Modern data science techniques are mostly probabilistic and naturally the outcomes of these techniques can only be evaluated with proper statistical thinking. Moreover, comparing with proper benchmarks is necessary for this evaluation.

Data processing and developing a machine learning model are two good examples that illustrate the unique challenges of data science.

Take a data processing task. You're a team lead and assign a week-long task to a data scientist on your team to create numerical features from some text data. The so-called word embeddings are a popular way of achieving this kind of task. Don't worry, we'll not dig deeper into the technical details of this. But rather, we want to highlight how working on this task can be a daunting one when it comes to evaluating its success. Next week, you review your teammate's work by visualizing the word embeddings she came up with through training an unsupervised machine learning model, and realize that some words aren't "that much good". Would you judge that the outcome of the task is a failure?

Well, no outcome can be perfect, especially when it comes to data science. And this is why we need to **compromise** between different objectives when evaluating the results. The usefulness of the word embeddings can only be assessed once they are fed into a machine learning model to solve a specific task. If the new embeddings help the success of that machine learning model, then the work should be regarded as a success.

However, training and evaluating a machine learning model is a later phase of the data science pipeline. If the project isn't at that phase, how can one judge the usefulness of this text processing work? As this simple example illustrates, evaluating the work that data scientists do requires a holistic vision that takes into account the big picture.

Evaluate a system as a whole

This leads us to the conclusion that we need to evaluate the success of a machine learning system as a whole. As we mentioned several times before, a data science project comprises of several stages, and many of these stages need several iterations. An experiment at a later stage can lead to an improvement in a former stage and vice versa. As in our text processing example, the success of a word embedding method should be measured based on its success in the machine learning task it helps to achieve.

Of course, a data science project isn't solely made up of machine learning processes. There are other phases like result communication, adding to the complexity of evaluating work done. These considerations are just a call to **flexibility** in evaluating the people and outcomes in the data science domain. If your background is from a field where metrics and outcomes are clearly defined and strictly maintained, then you need to adjust yourself to being more tolerant when judging outcomes.

Here are some useful suggestions when it comes to the evaluation of efforts and achievements in data science:

- We should be prepared to see results that are inferior to what was originally estimated. Estimating performance metrics is quite hard in data science. In addition, sometimes a shortfall in the value of success criterion means an improvement in the robustness of the system. In machine learning jargon, the best models are not those that achieve the highest value in a metric, but those that have a good balance between remembering what they learned and not being biased toward circumstances that they didn't see before—yes, we are talking about overfitting and generalization.

- When a data science project has started, we may see that progress is generally faster in the early stages. However, as time passes, we should be prepared to see that improvements in outcomes become slower and slower if there are any improvements at all.

- We shouldn't judge the quality of work in isolation. Instead, we should try to focus on the whole system.

These suggestions are just a short list of what can be done to better evaluate outcomes in data science. Note that we have only covered the context of a data science project but did not mention how to evaluate the performance of a data scientist. That's because evaluating a data scientist necessarily involves an evaluation of her work.

Next, we want to talk about some useful considerations in managing a data science team.

Let data scientists experiment

When it comes to increasing the chances of success of a data science project, one effective method that is commonly adopted is to encourage data scientists to experiment with different ideas and approaches. Data science is a rapidly evolving field. Technologies and the methods that are used in this field are also in a constant change. A method that everybody used a couple of years ago might be treated as an ineffective and archaic way today.

To ensure that a data science team can keep track of recent developments in the field, some incentives should be given to make the data scientists explore and learn by themselves. Among others, we list some incentives below.

- Organizing internal activities that facilitate the exchange of ideas is something we have observed more frequently in recent years. This could be something like an internal conference where different units in a company come together and share relevant information with each other. This kind of activity is useful for data scientists to interact with business units. Another activity could be a monthly technical meeting where people share new technologies they have used.

- Supporting contributions to open source projects is also something favorable in terms of the skills people gain on those experiments. These projects could be something related to data science or even something related to just software development and programming. Contributing to open source projects increases the collaboration skills of the contributors as well as providing a medium for the exchange of ideas and best practices across different companies and research groups. This is why many companies nowadays promote open source contributions.

- Budget for data scientists to attend external conferences and workshops for the professional development of team members. If chosen carefully, good conferences inform the attendants about new directions that the industry is taking and the technological changes that could impact the organization.

- Another effective incentive is to encourage them to write a technical blog. Writing is not something just for teaching but also a very effective way of learning. This blog could be something that is restricted to only company employees or could be something publicly accessible.

Learn by doing

Building toy projects or writing technical blog posts are great ways of learning. However, that doesn't suffice to make a data scientist more productive in their work. Providing a free space such that they can experiment on the work that they are doing is also beneficial. This not only fosters creativity, but also, as data science work requires a lot of experimentation, it can help generate ideas and skills for regular tasks.

Generalists versus specialists

The ongoing philosophical debate on whether someone should be a generalist or a specialist in the modern workplace also pertains to practitioners of data science. Working with great generalists is something that is precious in a data science project as data science is an interdisciplinary field and has components not just from the technical disciplines but also from business. That being said, specialization is also something valuable as the technical aspect of data science require intricate technical craftsmanship.

Although the choice of being a generalist or a specialist is a personal one, a corporate strategy is also necessary as it affects the human capital of the company. When a data scientist who is a generalist or a specialist leaves the company, the substitutes should ideally be put in place as fast as possible. Companies need to develop strategies for employee professional development such that every kind of personal profile can be found in the company when necessary. Although achieving a perfect balance is not feasible, a risk adverse management could mitigate the risk of losing an irreplaceable data scientist by investing in the professional development of all its employees. Doing so largely depends on finding the right balance in the generalist versus the specialist dilemma, by providing a third option, namely that of the versatilist. In this respect, we suggest two points that can help:

1. Don't assign a specific task to a single person if possible. Assigning a specific kind of task to a certain person would hinder the diffusion of knowledge in the team. While working on a specific field can make a person a good specialist, the risk of losing that person becomes more costly for the company. Working within a small group of two to three people not only makes teammates in that group share the knowledge more efficiently, it also minimizes the risk of losing critical employees.

2. Define a circulation strategy inside the data science teams. That is, make everyone in the team involved in every phase of the data science project where possible. Following this strategy would also foster "learning by doing", which eventually would result in better services and products.

Tips

It requires several years of professional experience to successfully evaluate data science projects and assess whether a data scientist is performing well. Remember that to keep your employees happy as well as productive, you need to give them enough free space so that they can follow their own technical development aspirations. This would make them own the things they are working on and hence increase their efficiency in their projects.

Key points

- Later phases in the data science pipeline can affect the success of the former phases and vice versa. Taking a holistic view is necessary when evaluating the results in each phase.

- Data science is a rapidly changing field. In order for data scientists to be on pace with recent developments, they need to experiment with the new technologies and methods.

- Learning by doing is a common way of keeping up to date with recent developments in data science. Some incentives should be given to data scientists so that they can experiment with new technologies and methods.

CHAPTER 10

Interview Highlights

We interviewed five different professionals in the field who were selected for their perspective and the insights they can offer. We carefully prepared a series of questions beforehand, tailored for the three different roles of these professionals: seasoned data scientists, directors involved in data science, and a data science talent acquisition specialist. The full interviews are in the appendix.

In this chapter we'll explore the highlights of these interviews as we attempt to form a narrative around the insights they yield. We'll look at the interview structure and advice the interviewees provided for those involved in data science.

Interview structure

The interviews were designed to be no more than 45 minutes long containing a few general questions followed by data science-related questions, next business-related questions, and finally asking for advice for data scientists or managers involved in data science projects.

Interview questions

The interview questions covered the following topics:

Work background

- Role in the organization
- Experience and knowledge of data science
- Domain expertise
- Important data science contributions
- Data science specialization
- Estimation of demand for data scientists
- Estimation of demand for AI professionals
- Rationale for specializing in data science recruiting

Data science and AI

- Skills and attributes sought in candidates
- How AI fits into data science
- Most promising aspects of data science
- Relevance of data science to different problems
- Building a data science team
- Opportunities for adding value to the organization through data science
- AI's role in adding value
- Remaining relevant as a data science or AI professional in a changing field
- Skills and qualities needed for data science work
- Most common data science skills encountered in data science positions

- Most common soft skills encountered in data science positions
- Value of the resume/CV in data science and AI recruiting
- Recommended platforms for data science and AI jobs

Business-related topics

- Gauging business acumen in candidates
- Processes automated or optimized through AI
- Relevance of domain knowledge in data science work
- Relevant business processes to data science work
- Data science projects with the highest ROI
- When an organization is data science-ready
- Organization's infrastructure in terms of data science work and readiness
- Differences in business understanding between junior- and senior-level data scientists
- Key skills and qualities for a business stakeholder in a data science project
- Types of companies that usually recruit data scientists and AI professionals
- How knowledgeable hiring managers are regarding data science and data science-related technologies
- Level of detail necessary for describing a data science position

Supplementary questions
- Advice to business people, regarding data science and AI
- Advice to data scientists, regarding the business

Note that not all of these were asked for each individual, since it made more sense to ask each interviewee questions more relevant to their role. For example, questions related to the demand of data science processionals were targeted towards the talent acquisition specialist only. Nevertheless, the main categories of the questions as well as the supplementary questions at the end remained the same across all interviewees. The idea is to have some common frame of reference across the various interviewees, while at the same time leveraging their role-related perspective.

Individuals interviewed

The individuals interviewed were selected from various organizations across different countries. The data scientists were Reza Dilmaghani (UK) and Veysel Kocaman (Netherlands), both senior-level data science professionals with a rich background in our field and a solid understanding of the business aspect of data science. Also, Veysel has recently undertaken a more managerial role in the company he works for in Amsterdam.

The directors were Brigham Hall (USA) and Daniel Pears (UK). While Brigham started as a data scientist, he is now a director in a healthcare company in Boston, MA. Both of these individuals have a solid understanding of data science and have experience working with all sorts of data professionals, in different industries. Last but not least, we have a data science talent acquisition specialist, Chris Wright (UK), who has a lengthy experience as a technical talent acquisition specialist, with a specialization in data science and AI, having placed many data scientists and other data-related professionals in various organizations in the greater London area.

Data science-specific material

The main aspects related to the information acquired from the questionnaires have to do with the skills and attributes of data scientists, the experience involved in getting to a senior-level or managerial position, the contribution of data science in an organization, the building of a data science team, and AI's role in adding value.

Skills and attributes

Regarding skills and attributes, there is a consensus regarding data scientist technical competence—software engineering, algorithms, critical reasoning, statistics, the ability to clean the data properly, and having a good coding style. Interestingly, no interviewee mentioned anything about a data science or even a computer science degree. In fact, one of them said that he values experience in different domains, something that's often aligned with shifting disciplines on one's journey towards data science.

In addition, in the interviews there are references to "being able to build a reliable model and optimize it is a recurring pattern," just like "being able to handle different kinds of models, instead of sticking to a couple of them that you know well." This model diversity is something few people talk about, even though it deserves a lot of attention, since it enables you to gain a deeper understanding of the craft and develop the data science mindset. Also, being familiar with different statistical packages and programming platforms is considered to be a plus.

What's more, project management was something that came up as a useful skill. This is particularly important in senior-level roles, although all kinds of data scientists can benefit. Not everyone mentioned this, but it was implied since it has to do with understanding how business works and how work rhythms can be aligned.

Domain knowledge is a big one, since people from different roles brought it up as a prerequisite of good data science work.

Finally, soft skills like communication, especially listening and understanding what the customer is saying, are something of a recurring theme too. This is particularly important for senior-level positions where liaising with the customer is part of the job and tailoring existing know-how to different problems is expected.

Experience

The amount of experience required depends on the role; you can get a data science job with much less experience than ten years, if you know your data science well. However, for a senior-level or director position, ten years seems to be the minimum amount of experience required.

Value of data science

Data science has contributed significantly to the organizations of the people interviewed. For business people, data science's contribution had to do with KPIs changing in the desired direction, or with the optimization of behind-the-scenes tasks like cloud or big data. From a data scientist's perspective, being able to frame business problems well and figure out solutions was the most important contribution. Also, generating or acquiring data while keeping a human in the loop ensures a certain quality standard. Also, building smart algorithms to create something meaningful out of the data, was something essential as a contribution, particularly for a start-up setting.

Building a data science team

In order to build a data science team, the business people interviewed had some interesting ideas. One of them suggested an approach consisting of hiring the following kinds of people:

- a strong generalist, someone with competence in various aspects of data science, though still having some specialization, such as in communication

- another generalist

- a data engineer

- a "data story-teller" for handling the last-mile problem of connecting the dots and presenting a coherent story to the project stakeholders

Note that the term generalist includes a certain can-do attitude, which is essential for handling a broad range of aspects of data science work.

The other suggested approach was of having a project-specific team, consisting of specialists that are most suitable for the particular challenges of that project. For example, if there is a lot of text involved, get NLP-oriented data scientists onboard. After the project is done, these people can get involved in company labs, where they can work on other data science-related tasks, until they can be absorbed in another relevant project.

Note that the approach of hiring a bunch of data scientists regardless of their specialization or outsourcing the hiring task to a data science lead were both found to be inadequate.

AI's role

Naturally, AI plays an important role in all this, especially nowadays. In some cases, the focus was on particular AI technologies, such as Keras and TensorFlow, or systems— such as CNNs, LSTMs, and chatbots—and how they can aid classification or other kinds of predictive analytics. In another case, it was all about natural language understanding, NLP, and text generation.

The most interesting response was definitely the growing importance of business understanding. The recruited data scientists should be able to explain why their solutions are a more efficient way to perform more high-level processes that a human would. This is expected to change hiring through the merging of the business analyst role with the data scientist one.

Remaining relevant

The interviewees said a few things about other data science-related matters. For example, the most promising aspects of the field, according to the interviewees were:

- The democratization of data science know-how and how it will advance its evolution as a discipline.

- The optimization of resource-heavy processes like Extract-Transfer-Load (ETL) through data science.

- Communication and liaising with the business.

- Automation, particularly through AI.

The relevance of data science in one's work is also something we examined, particularly when asking business people. In one case, multi-classification problems were used to target customers more effectively. This application of data science demonstrates that even a fairly simple use of data science can yield valuable concrete results. In another case, data science was used for complaint analysis, developing intelligent frameworks for ensuring better data quality, and for using chatbots internally, such as for improved communications within the organization as in service desk requests.

Remaining relevant as the field changes is something the data scientists interviewed had something to say about. Namely, both of the data scientists interviewed suggested reading technical articles, though the sources and type of articles varied quite a bit. One of them also mentioned publishing articles. University work was something both data scientists talked about too, since teaching is considered a good way to stay up-to-date. One of the interviewees stressed the value of listening to podcasts, mentoring, recruiting agencies even when not looking for a new job, and attending various data science events on Meetup.

Business-specific material

The interviews yielded lots of material on business-related topics too. Specifically, we gathered information about business acumen in data scientists, domain knowledge and its importance, business processes related to data science, and when an organization is data science-ready.

Business acumen

As regards to business acumen, the interviewees offered a variety of insights. In most cases, it was considered essential, for various reasons, while in one case it was a "nice to have." The reason for the latter response was domain-specific; acumen could be gained easily through reading MBA blogs, for instance.

In one other case, business acumen was aligned with industry knowledge or specific business-related scenarios that were used to gauge the data scientist's grasp of the business world. For instance, it involves understanding the degree of commerciality of a data science project and discerning how long it would take before a project is acceptable, instead of getting stuck in a loop geared towards perfection.

Business acumen was also framed as the discerning factor between the seasoned data scientist and the beginner in the craft. The data scientists who answered this question mentioned experience, understanding of how an organization or sector works, where various data science tools are applicable, problem-solving when it comes to business problems, understanding how a model affects the business, and being able to see the bigger picture.

Domain knowledge

Domain knowledge is an important topic regarding the business aspect of data science and the interviewees shared some interesting ideas. The general consensus was that domain knowledge is very important in data science, particularly in certain industries. In these cases, it's distinguished from business acumen, as it has more to do with internal knowledge of an industry that can be leveraged to make better use of the data involved.

In healthcare, specifically, it is crucial and there is a steep learning curve, while without it, you can't do much as a data scientist. Getting subject matter experts (SMEs) in the team and reading healthcare blogs, however, can help remedy this.

Also, in the customer services area, domain knowledge is useful but only for medium- and senior-level positions. After all, junior-level data scientists work alongside with a senior-level one, so they can be guided.

The data scientists interviewed concurred with the previous view, though one of them added that domain knowledge is useful in the business side of the projects, while the other one said that it is something required during data preparation, which couldn't be done properly without understanding the domain.

Business processes related to data science

As for the business processes related to data science, one of the interviewees said that CRMs are typical processes that are related to data science, as they can be made more efficient, improving the effectiveness of the sales funnel. This is possible through predictive analytics models, such as multi-class classifiers. The other interviewee mentioned that all business processes lend themselves to data science.

This is due to the fact that they have evolved so that they are at the same level as analytics tools.

Data science readiness

But when is an organization data science-ready? That's a question the interviewees shed some light on. Namely, it's really all about the data, though the stakeholders' understanding of data science is also a factor. Particularly, having sufficient data of decent quality that's also easily accessible seems to be a must, while having some procedures to share the data can be quite useful too. However, to make this happen, they need to start acquiring data way before hiring any data scientists to ensure there is going to be enough data available when the time comes. It's important to note though that the people involved in this pipeline are better off being knowledgeable about data science, so that they collect useful data and store it efficiently. Additionally, open-mindedness and the ability to think outside the box are very useful for the stakeholders involved.

Facilitating business decisions

Interviewees mentioned that many people don't think about the key skills and qualities for a business person who's a stakeholder for a data science project.

One of the data scientists interviewed mentioned that a general understanding of data science buzzwords is a good place to start, while intelligence to see where using data science would result in a more efficient solution is also very useful. Additionally, being able to define the problem accurately, is a big plus, particularly when it is a very specific problem that's different from the standard ones most common in the field.

The other data scientist went into more length about some more specific things, such as the fact that these systems developed in a data science project are there to facilitate business decisions, not replace humans. Also, not trusting every good result, especially when the data isn't enough or of poor quality. In addition, not trusting charts fully is a good trait to have, especially since the data these charts come from is often not referenced. Furthermore, if there isn't sufficient or reliable enough data, they shouldn't initiate a machine learning or AI-related project, as it's doubtful the corresponding models will be reliable.

Regarding hiring managers, they are generally quite knowledgeable about data science. However, you may still come across someone who doesn't know much about data science, so you have to be aware of this possibility. This can potentially become apparent from the specs of a data scientist position, since the requirements listed tend to reflect their knowledge of the field. People who have something particular in mind and who know what data science can offer, tend to have more specific requirements, while others who just want to hire a data scientist because other companies do, tend to have more generic specs.

Tips

Last but not least, the interviewees were happy to provide us with some good advice, regardless of our roles as data science-related professionals. Let's examine these in more detail.

Tips for data scientists

One of the interviewees stressed how data science is a pragmatic journey, highlighting the need of the data scientist's work to be relevant to the business. Having the right mindset for data science is another a key point. Another one of the interviewees added that the business-first mentality is "an expected capability" nowadays instead of a "nice to have." Business acumen and humility were the most important things to keep in mind, according to another interviewee, along with an urge to improve productivity.

The interviewees agreed that knowing business practices was essential, since being a one-dimensional data scientist doesn't do anyone any favors. One of the data scientists elaborated a bit more on this point, stressing the need of understanding the business problem, asking many questions, and gaining an understanding of the domain.

Tips for business people

One of the interviewees put forward the idea of fewer meetings, since avoiding daily meetings and giving data scientists the space to explore can yield more benefits in the long run. Also, remembering that data science projects don't always yield immediate value is very useful. Another interviewee suggested that basic data literacy is certainly going to become a fundamental requirement to anyone working in the industry, so understanding how to interpret the data is going to be a crucial business skill, while the days of being opinion-rich and data-poor are coming to an end. Keeping an open mind and getting someone who has a positive personality are things another interviewee suggested. Finding people who know data science is easy, but it's best to look for someone who can simplify complexity who thinks outside the box, as such a person is bound to make a bigger impact.

Another interviewee put forward the suggestion of not fearing that they will be replaced by AI. Instead, we should all understand that data scientists are trying to improve the organizations' efficiency and reduce costs through data science. Finally, an interviewee suggested that there should be more focus on data engineering, in order to avoid getting stuck when building a data model. Also, having role-specific people for certain data science roles is something worth considering, since there is rarely a one-size-fits-all solution for human resources in data science.

Key points

Let's now take a look at some useful considerations to have about these topics covered in the interviews, and regarding this method of acquiring information in general. Overall, everyone had lots of things to say about this subject but as we needed to keep the interviews to a manageable length, out of respect of the interviewees' time, we limited the questions to the particular categories mentioned.

Regarding interviews as a tool, they are a tried and tested way of acquiring useful information about something, particularly when it comes to specific and practical experience. It's no wonder that it is also the technique still used in evaluating candidates, as we saw in a previous chapter. However, special care must be taken in coming up with relevant questions as well as in ensuring the interviewee fully comprehends what you are inquiring.

CHAPTER 11

Educational Resources

In this chapter we'll explore the various options when it comes to educational resources, some criteria you can use for discerning the most reliable ones, the best options for educational resources for data science and AI, depending on your role, and some other useful considerations.

Selecting educational resources

Educational resources are essential for keeping up with the latest developments in data science and AI as these fields are constantly changing. What's more, there is a large variety of tools used for data science tasks and it's difficult to gauge what's relevant enough to be useful. Unfortunately, many information sources are unreliable or incomplete, so special care must be taken when picking a resource for this purpose. This applies both to someone working as a data scientist and someone managing a data science division.

The value of proper educational resources lies in the quality of the material available. With the democratization of technical knowledge came the inevitable drop in quality. However, this is not an insurmountable issue and there are viable strategies for selecting trustworthy resources and using them effectively in your data science or AI learning.

Types of educational resources

There are various types of educational resources when it comes to data science and AI. In the following diagram (Fig. 6), you can see a taxonomy of the most important types.

Figure 6. General taxonomy of the most important and widely used educational resources for data science and AI

The value of each of these resources depends upon the target audience. In general, books appeal more to serious learners who wish to go into some depth on a topic, videos for people who want to get a general idea before they delve deeper and who have limited time, and tutorials and hands-on projects are aimed at people who want to learn specific practical things about certain methods.

As you may suspect, these different resource types have different purposes. High-level books are better for getting an understanding of the topic and developing the right mindset, while hands-on books are geared towards technique. Demo videos are better for understanding why something is used, while explanatory videos can teach the justification for a method. As for tutorials and hands-on projects, the method-focused variety is better for helping the learner understand how a particular methodology works in practice. Complementary to these, the application-focused ones are ideal for depicting how a known methodology is useful for specific scenarios. Ideally someone would use all of these throughout his career.

In a data science or AI course, you generally encounter all of these mediums. Of course, how much depth you want to go into depends on your role, since a manager, for example, doesn't need to know the ins and outs of the various methods, but a data scientist or an AI expert would need to know about the methods.

Criteria for selecting an educational resource

But how exactly does one select an educational resource to use, be it for getting the know-how to become a data scientist or for learning enough about the field to work with data scientists? As the time required to go through many of these resources is substantial, it's best to make an effort to prioritize, otherwise you may end up wasting a lot of time and effort. So, we recommend that you employ at least a few of the following criteria in making your decision:

- Criteria based on content creator:
    - Education level of the content creator
    - Experience, especially related to the creation of educational content
    - Charisma or style of the content creator

- Criteria related to the content itself:
    - Breadth of coverage
    - Depth of coverage for more specialized resources
    - Applicability of the material

- Theme-related criteria:
    - Primary focus
    - Connection to business aspect of the craft
    - Use of comprehensive examples

- Additional criteria:

- o References used
- o Price of the resource
- o Time required to find the resource
- o Other factors

Beyond these criteria, there are others that may be more domain-specific, such as the resource's relevance to a particular field, such as e-commerce, or the data involved. Nevertheless, this list of criteria can shed some light as to what is worth your while, helping you discern the most suitable educational resources from the less useful ones.

Educational resources to avoid

Although which educational resources you select depends on your own set of requirements and constraints, there are some useful rules of thumb about which ones you are better off avoiding altogether.

For instance, resources that are free are generally not a good alternative for a number of reasons. Apart from the fact that they usually don't have any quality control, they also are often developed as a vanity project of the content creator, who at the same time won't usually have much experience in creating educational material. What's more, there are so many such resources available that finding one that is marginally good enough is a time-consuming project not worth your time.

On the other side of the spectrum, resources that are developed quickly and for the primary purpose of making money—for example, most YouTube videos and most projects from subscription-based publishers—are also not a viable option. That's not to say that all of these educational resources are bad, but the good ones are few and finding them can be quite challenging. Also, they generally lack the professionalism of other resources, created by more serious authors.

Finally, resources that are too academic, although they may be useful for university students, are not at all useful for industry. This is partly because they focus too much on techniques rather than applications. They can also be more detail-focused, making it difficult for someone unprepared to get something useful out of them. Still, if you are used to this sort of material, academic resources (as for example textbooks) may add to your learning.

Options for educational resources

Educational resources for data science

When it comes to data science, there is a plethora of options out there for educational resources. From books to videos to tutorials, the range is large. However, before you delve into any one, it's best to organize them in terms of their objectives and think about what's more necessary for you or your teammates at this particular time and to prioritize them.

Namely, the key educational resources in data science are largely dependent on what your role is exactly. So, based on that, you may want to explore the following options, ranked in terms of relevance:

If you are a practitioner within a data science team:

- Books, particularly those related to more specialized methods, for niche know-how you wish to cultivate

- Videos, especially those delving deeper into the concepts explored

- Tutorials, particularly those dealing with essential methodologies used in data science projects

- Hands-on projects, especially those related to newly learned methods

- Conferences on data science and programming

If you are a team lead for a data science team:

- Books, particularly those related to the bigger picture or specialized methods

- Videos, especially those delving into high-level topics and leadership

- Conferences on data science and programming, particularly domain-specific ones

- Hands-on projects, especially whenever a leadership role is required

If you are a manager involved in data science projects:

- Videos, especially those delving into high-level topics and leadership

- Some specialized books, dealing with data science from a business perspective

- Conferences on data science, particularly domain-specific ones

Educational resources for AI

As AI has boomed over the past few years, the options in this area are quite vast too. Although most of them are focused on some very particular aspects of AI, you can find other, less specialized educational resources too. Yet, like in data science work, which resources are most suitable for you depends on your role in these AI-related projects. Here are our recommendations, ranked in terms of relevance.

If you are a normal member of an AI team:

- Tutorials, particularly those dealing with essential systems used in AI-related projects

- Videos, especially those delving deeper into the concepts explored, while helping develop an intuition of the systems described

- Books, particularly those exploring different frameworks and systems

- Hands-on projects, especially those related to newly learned methods

- Conferences on AI and programming

If you are a team lead for an AI team:

- Videos, especially those delving into high-level topics and computational resource management

- Books, particularly those related to the bigger picture or specialized systems like domain-specific applications

- Conferences on AI and programming, particularly application-oriented ones

- Hands-on projects, especially whenever a leadership role is required

If you are a manager involved in AI projects:

- Videos, especially those delving into high-level topics and leadership

- Conferences on AI, particularly application-oriented ones

- Some specialized books, dealing with AI from a business perspective

General educational resources

Some educational resources are more general and often have more to do with specific tools or, conversely, with the mindset needed for the process of analyzing data. For example, any book, video, or tutorial on a programming language usable in data science or AI would be a potentially useful resource to consider. Such languages are Julia, Python, Scala, and to some extent R, though the latter's applicability in AI is somewhat questionable. These educational resources are particularly useful for the more hands-on professionals within these fields.

What's more, conferences in these areas, even if they are more geared towards a particular programming language, can be a great educational resource too—for example, the JuliaCon conference for the Julia language. However, the role of such a resource is more supplementary since it's doubtful that you can learn the fundamentals of data science or AI at such a conference. Still, you may be able to pick up some useful ideas as well as get a better understanding of how certain methods are applied to specific problems. Often the people participating in these conferences are seasoned professionals and have a great deal to share, so networking with them is an added bonus to the educational benefit of the conference.

Finally, certain data science and AI meetups are also worth considering, particularly those organized by independent professionals in these fields. Such events can be more accessible than most conferences, while they are significantly more frequent, and sometimes equally educational. Although most of these meetups are geared towards hands-on professionals, they can sometimes appeal to those in leadership roles too.

Tips

When selecting and using an educational resource for data science and AI, there are some useful things to keep in mind, in order to make the most out of that resource. First of all, a resource that may be ideal for one individual may be substandard for another one, even if they share the same criteria.

In addition, easier doesn't necessarily mean better when it comes to data science educational resources. If you have an aversion to challenging material, perhaps you are better off seeking help through a consultant or a good mentor. Also, some of the material may be easier than the more advanced stuff people often talk about lately, but you can't rely on the easy stuff only if you want to do something useful with data science or AI. This is particularly valid for hands-on professionals in these fields.

Moreover, it would be best to be skeptical about expedited courses on data science and AI, promising sufficient expertise in these areas within 10 weeks, even if you're a beginner in programming. These boot camps are generally fairly shallow and too focused on technique, while they care more about the revenue they can make from their students than any pedagogical outcome. Naturally, not all of the data science and AI courses out there are useless, but unless you have internalized the data science mindset, it's doubtful they are going to help you much, at least not enough to be worth the money you spend on them. Besides, their role is more supplementary than anything else, regardless of how they are marketed.

Furthermore, understanding the business aspect of data science and AI is a long process that cannot be learned just through a few educational resources. Such an endeavor requires a lot of contemplation on real-world problems, fruitful discussions with people adept in the field, and a great deal of practice. A good book or video may help, but it's doubtful that it will make you an expert in this or any other arcane aspect of the craft.

Finally, it's best to make use of a variety of educational resources in your data science learning efforts. Videos, for example are particularly good and they convey a lot of information in little time, but you'll usually need something more substantial too if you want to optimize your learning of the field. After all, unless they go in-depth on the topics they delve into, their role is usually supplementary too, just like most tutorials out there. That's why every content creator worth her salt would advise you to practice everything you learn, in order to understanding concepts in depth and learn to apply them, whether it is something hands-on or more high-level.

Key points

- The rapid growth of the fields of data science and AI has made any reliable education in them challenging, while the vast amount of options has turned the choice of resource to use into a daunting task.

- The value of proper educational resources lies in the quality of the material available, something that may not be as easy to gauge without a set of criteria covering different aspects of these resources.

- There are various types of educational resources when it comes to data science and AI, such as books (high-level and hands-on), videos (demos and explanatory), and tutorials and hands-on projects (method-focused and application-focused).

- Each type of educational resource has its advantages, though it is best to make use of a variety, since they generally complement each other. Courses are one way of effectively accomplishing that.

- There are various criteria for selecting an appropriate educational resource for your data science or AI learning, such as the experience of the content creator, particularly in content creation, the applicability of the material, the focus of the resource, and the resource's price.

- Certain resources are best avoiding, such as free or freemium resources, resources designed for easy money-making for their creators, and resources that are too academic.

CHAPTER 12

Putting it Together

Abundant information about the technical aspects of data science can be found in many platforms. However, information about the business aspect of the craft isn't as accessible, even as it is becoming more important. Complementing technical capabilities with a strong sense of business and good domain knowledge is of primary concern for the data scientist of the future. This is what motivated us to write this book.

We know that covering every important aspect of a discipline—even if it were possible—is something beyond the scope of this book. Thus, throughout the book, we touched upon many points that seem important to us. We tried to cover topics as diverse as possible so that our readers can get a holistic view of data science and data science professionals.

This chapter recaps the important points in the book to act as a cheat sheet for your future reference.

The confusion between data science and AI

One important clarification we made in the beginning of this book is that data science and artificial intelligence are two separate disciplines with their own methodologies and toolkits. Despite their different goals and perspectives, data science makes use of AI technologies when doing so adds value to a data science project or product.

Knowing the difference between the two disciplines is important in terms of the following:

- A data scientist can organize her way of thinking and invest in the right technologies and tools to enhance her career. If someone's goal is to conquer the finance universe, then learning autonomous driving technologies would be the wrong place to invest time. Our concern is that the hype around AI, especially in the mainstream media, can mislead data science professionals in choosing what to learn next.

- A person who is working in a business unit, on the other hand, can distinguish between the capabilities of data science and AI so that she can align her expectations with the data science or AI team. This point is especially crucial for executives. In order to set achievable goals, knowing the capabilities of data science and AI is necessary.

Without misreading developments in both fields, management can set feasible objectives that are within the scope of data science and AI teams.

How AI fits in the whole picture

We provided a brief review of how data science benefits from AI methods. Specifically, we underlined that AI techniques have evolved dramatically in the last decade thanks to the deep learning revolution. Data science especially makes use of AI methods when it comes to working with complex data like text, speech, image, and video.

The most common scenarios where data science uses AI techniques, especially deep learning methods, occur when working with these complex data types. Natural language processing and computer vision are two areas where data science projects regularly use AI. Specifically, when turning textual data into numerical representations, data scientists might use word embedding methods from the natural language processing literature. When it comes to creating useful representational features of the images and the videos, data science uses computer vision techniques that are based on deep learning methods.

This is why we suggest data scientists train in the fundamentals of deep learning. We emphasized that data science and artificial intelligence are two disciplines that have their own research programs and agendas. That being said, a capable data scientist wouldn't hesitate to use methods from AI when the need arises.

Business-savvy data scientist

The superstar of this book is a well-rounded data science professional who we call the business-savvy data scientist. A precious asset for a company, this ideal figure creates value where she works as well as for the teammates with whom she works. The important characteristics of this professional are:

- Technically knowledgeable.

- Adaptable to new circumstances and to new technologies.

- Competency in transforming business questions into data science questions and solving them in the context of data science.

- Great communication skills in the sense of team collaboration as well as with project stakeholders from other disciplines.

- Flexible when confronting problems that are sub-optimally solved with traditional approaches—easily coming to compromises and solutions.

- Natural mentor who helps other colleagues learn new things, skillful in networking not just in the company but also with the outside world.

- Aptitude for research and trying novel ways to solve a specific task—even better, demonstrated creativity.

- Great at time management and reporting results to relevant stakeholders.

The list above constitutes the profile of a technical professional who would be a great asset for any company. Finding this kind of person isn't something trivial. Likewise, striving for this profile is a great investment for any data scientist.

How data science transforms business

Digital transformation will stay at the top of the agenda for every kind of company for some time yet. Innovations in products, services, and business models urge even long-established companies to transform their way of doing business in order to maintain their presence in a competitive environment.

Data science is the main driver of this dynamic environment. Now companies are going through data-driven transformation in every sector including centuries old finance, automotive, retail, and relatively new ones like cyber security and software development.

Data scientists work as the facilitators and catalysts of this process. Data scientists with strong business acumen can shed light on the value that data-driven transformation can bring to their companies.

To illustrate how data-driven innovations change businesses, we gave a brief case study from finance. Interesting enough, an old industry like finance is among the pioneers of adopting data-driven innovations due to the data involved in this sector, which qualifies as big data. From chatbots to fully autonomous banking, the finance sector exhibits a good example of the rapid and widespread use of digital transformation.

Hiring data scientists

Human capital is probably the most important asset a company can hold in its portfolio. Being aware of this fact, hiring the right talent for data science teams is something that is critical for the success of data science projects and digital transformation efforts.

An ideal data science candidate is someone who can combine technical mastery with business acumen. Data scientists with solid domain knowledge are in high demand across different industries. However, finding and hiring such an individual is not easy. These candidates are scarce and hence, most of the time, in the hiring process, some sort of compromise is necessary. The hiring process involves one or more of the following evaluation methods, and ideally all of them:

1. Initial phone screening
2. Live online coding challenge
3. A take-home machine learning task
4. Personal interview

Using this framework, both technical capacities as well as domain knowledge can be evaluated and hence the right person can be hired.

How to manage a data science project

The most common project management frameworks across the industries are Agile methodologies. Among several Agile approaches, the scrum framework is the leading one in terms of adoption rate. For this reason, most data science teams are working with the scrum framework. However, fitting a data science project into the scrum framework has several challenges. Among them are the iterative nature of the data science pipeline and difficulties in estimating performance metrics in advance. To better handle a data science project using the scrum framework, we proposed several guidelines including:

- Create the backlog by taking into consideration the consecutive phases of a standard data science pipeline.

- Create tasks that are as small as possible to deal with ambiguities and unknowns.

- Use a simple versioning method to deal with the possible iterations of a task.

- If your role in the project is the scrum master, be prepared for missing deadlines for some tasks, especially at the beginning of the project.

- If your role in the project is product owner, be prepared that outcomes that were targeted at the beginning of a project might have to be dropped as the project progresses.

Understanding the limitations of the scrum framework and the peculiarities of a data science project is necessary for a well-functioning data science team.

Evaluating and managing data scientists

When it comes to managing a team of data scientists, one big challenge to overcome is how to evaluate the work of team members. Iterative phases in a typical data science pipeline make it hard to measure the success of a task without looking at the big picture. To be able to better manage a data science team, we mentioned the importance of a holistic view that should be adopted when evaluating the work of data scientists.

Another challenge we talked about is how to increase the productivity of data scientists as well as how to enhance their technical knowledge. Data science is changing rapidly and it can be challenging to keep up with recent developments. In order to motivate data scientists, we emphasized giving free space to them where they can experiment with their own ideas.

Educational resources

One other important aspect of the professional development of any data scientist is education in the craft. Data science technologies, especially AI, are changing so fast, such that keeping up the pace is almost impossible especially for someone who has many tasks to deliver every day. Still, lagging behind the state-of-the-art technologies and methods is a great risk to the development of a data scientist as a professional. To this end, we categorized the three types of resources that one can use to keep learning: books, videos, and tutorials. We highlighted the advantages of each type of educational resource, while stressing that a variety is preferable, since they generally complement each other.

Key points

As we're ending this book, we hope that we have given a holistic view of data science with a focus on its business side. To accompany our treatment of the craft, we have provided the opportunity for our readers to meet with professionals of the field through interviews. To this end, we conducted several interviews with the professionals to give our readers a sense of how different aspects of data science are implemented in the industry. We hope that these interviews, found in the following appendix, will be helpful in terms of their insights and practicality.

Interviews

Brigham Hall

Q1: What's your role exactly in the organization you are part of?

Initially I was the principal data scientist and now it has evolved to being the director of data science for a healthcare company. This really means that I'm a player coach. I still do a lot of coding but a larger portion of my time is spent in two other buckets: coaching junior analysts with best practices, and to solve that last-mile problem: trying to land analytics with the executives as well as our advisory board.

I would say around 50% coding and the other 50% communicating and liaising [with business people].

Q2: How long have you acquired data science knowledge for?

That's a good question because the field is so fuzzy about what data science is. It really started during my time as a research fellow at Boston University School of Management in Organizational Behavior. There we would study how teams worked together to succeed or conversely fail, especially the latter. To do so, we had videos of a number of volunteer teams. As you know video is basically unstructured data and as researchers we had to figure out how to take video and turn it into a spreadsheet, so that we could analyze it. At the time I don't think we were using the term "Data Science" to explain what we were doing, but that was part of the job. So, that's where I believe I started and if you add all that time up, it's probably shy of 10 years.

Q3: What's your domain expertise?

I'm thinking of the "capital T" skill shape that a lot of people talk about, where the crown of the T is all the skills you know and the body of the T is your specialty. My specialty has been communication. I'm particularly good at being the liaison between data scientists who are much smarter than me and executives who are also much smarter than me in their respective domains, and being that connective tissue. So, communication has been my key strength and it's a soft skill set, one that I think data scientists should think about more, since communication is key.

Q4: What's the most important contribution of data science in your organization?

Data science here is very pragmatic, so it's not meaningful to dazzle the executives with the latest and greatest algorithms, it does not dazzle them to spend months working on a problem. What impresses them is fast iteration, making sure they have line-of-sight of the work, not going down a rabbit hole into a cave and not sharing your work for months, and where the rubber hits the road, we really need to see the KPIs pop. So it's all very pragmatic and we measure certain business KPIs and expect the investment in data science to manifest itself into more profitability.

Q5: What skills and attributes do you seek in a data scientist you hire?

So, this is something that I first authored for our pillars for the team here, and these are things I see as an evolving practice because we are basically new to this. We follow six pillars that I suggested and those pillars are software engineering, algorithms, data, model formulation, project management, and communication (last mile problem). The last three tend to suffer for most data scientists encountered. Also, the hypothesis-driven approach tends to be absent, in my opinion. Instead of plugging in Random Forests or some other model, I like to write down 20-30 questions that would help the business and just believe that if I had a magic wand and I knew the answers to those questions, I could bring a lot of value, and I believe that's what begins the journey for doing analytics in a business setting.

Q6: How does AI fit in the whole data science work, in your domain?

When I think of AI, I think of Deep Learning, Convolutional Neural Networks, and LSTMs. In our practice, because our work touches operations quite a bit, there are opportunities to use Keras and TensorFlow, and CNNs and LSTMs, as multi-classifiers for the work that we do. So, those are tools that we are exploring right now, though currently we tend to use the traditional canonical classification approaches like Random Forests that many people use.

Q7: What aspects of data science, in general, do you find most promising right now?

The thing that really excites me is democratization and the open-source movement around data science. Those traditional barriers for innovation have disappeared and I would just imagine the velocity of the evolution of data science is going to increase exponentially.

Q8: When do you find data science most relevant to a problem you are tackling?

We are a data broker who works with health insurance companies to find members that are better suited for municipal or social security benefits. So what happened was that there was a misclassification of certain members, and if we could use classifiers to find these members by looking at their electronic health records and the data that we have, then we put them in the right bucket. So it's a win-win in the sense that we get a finders' fee for doing so and our partners are helped fiscally because we moved those members to municipal plans that are now serving the members with better care.

Data science affects that since a lot of what we do is classification. That's the biggest pain point. So we have a call center and those business owners and their respective PNLs are really focused on the screening rate, so when we have a false positive, meaning that we call a healthy person who doesn't need our services, we wasted their time and the time of our member advocates. We can quantify that, so our charter here, our primary charter in addition to building the culture, is to reduce the false positives and increase our true positives. It's really good since the organization gives us a blank check to do that: they haven't put any barriers as to what algorithms we can use but the flip side of that is that they expect results from what we do.

Q9: How would you build a data science team for a project?

I guess I should start with me, as a first hire. Why would I be a good first hire? I'm a strong generalist [versatilist]: I don't specialize in anything beyond communication, I could do end-to-end projects very well without having dependencies on dev ops, DB folks, etc. I could move very quickly just working by myself because I'm a blend of a data scientist and a consultant, so I'm good at really getting down to the true business problems and then wrangling the data and then landing the insights, by myself. The second hire would be a generalist as well. I think having two generalists is a strong approach to building a good team at the beginning. By generalist I mean a can-do attitude. After the second hire that's where we need some specializing. It would be helpful at that point to get a data engineer. So, one thing I'm not particularly good at is automation, something like Apache Airflow, but that's something a data engineer can do. Of course, all the feature engineering is something that the data engineer can also do. So, I'd hire two generalists, a data engineer, and at that point a "data story-teller" to handle the last-mile problem and serve as a management liaison. That's not a person who comes from an engineering background. In our case we have someone who was trained as a journalist, for example.

Q10: How do you gauge business acumen in a data science candidate?

I'm thinking of the classical Venn diagram about what is data science, with the three rings. In my opinion, I agree that business acumen is an important pillar, but it's not exactly the primary thing I look for in a candidate. I'm looking for adequate coding skills and statistical understanding in the forefront and the business acumen thing is a "nice to have" because that's something you can train on the job with. I would imagine this would be totally different for someone in investment banking or a consulting firm, but here our business understanding is quite minimal. You need to understand probability metrics like PNL, and other metrics, as well as how they can affect the bottom line. Parallel to that they also need to have an interest in the industry, I think that's important. You don't need to be an MBA, but it would be nice if the candidates spend a weekend reading up on those mini-MBA blogs to get up to speed.

Q11: What process do you normally opt to automate or optimize through AI?

That's what I'm trying to figure out right now. The reason for automation is that every month our partners send us fresh data. So clearly there is an opportunity to refresh our models but more importantly we need to score our members for operations. This is a monthly cadence and right now this is handled through coding notebooks manually, so there is a ripe opportunity to optimize that. Also, we serve dozens of partners so the problem grows. As for the optimization piece, we are beginning to look at ensemble modeling.

Q12: How relevant is domain knowledge for a data scientist in your area?

Huge! I've been here shy of two years and I feel I've only touched the tip of the iceberg for healthcare. So, taking a step back and looking at all the industries where data science has landed well, tech and manufacturing companies were low-hanging fruits, while what has not been touched yet, in my opinion, are education, construction, and healthcare. It turns out there is a reason: the data is disparate and even standardization of codes is sometimes not agreed upon by different governing bodies. So, in terms of domain knowledge, there is a high learning curve in healthcare and I think the two tactics to solve that are: hire SMEs, which we've done, and read healthcare blogs and understand what the space is all about.

Q13: What business processes do you find more relevant to data science work?

CRM comes to mind, because I'd done work with CRMs before my current employer, as well as a little bit in Microsoft. So, CRM is your customer relationship management, but basically it's the sales funnel that is important. The idea is that if you have maybe 100 prospects you are not going to sell a product or a service to those 100 prospects; it's going to go through a funnel and through that some will fall out of the funnel, so maybe by the end of the day you only reach five of those people, but if you model that correctly you have a lot of opportunities to intervene with folks to increase that yield. You also have a lot of opportunities to understand the customer journey and it's just such a rich area. So, I'd say that in terms of business processes if you are in operations or marketing, it is time to understand the CRM process and also understand customer segmentation. What marketeers understand as your customers, prior to using data science, that's always useful to know.

Q14: Which data science projects do you find yield the highest ROI?

There are so many. It's relevant to the business need. We are not process- or technology- or algorithm-centric, we are just solutions-oriented so I feel that this needs to be catered in the business. I think data scientists should challenge and poke and really catalyze this discussion about what is value in the business, and that will dictate the answer. Here, in our case, this is multi-classification.

Q15: What advice would you give to data scientists, regarding the business aspect of things?

In my personal practice, being a data scientist is a pragmatic journey. So, the work you need to do needs to be relevant to the business. That mindset is a good place to start for data scientists, particularly if they came from a research background. So, setting expectations and line-of-sight would be helpful opportunities for data scientists to think about. That touches the communications management part I was speaking about earlier. This way your internal champion can cheer-lead for you and your final presentation is not a big reveal but something more-or-less known, since you've been meeting so many times.

Q16: What advice would you give to business people, regarding data science and AI?

Fewer meetings; don't try to meet with data scientists every day, give them space to explore. This is a journey so you might not see ROI for 6 or 12 months, that's something you really need to think about before you place your bets but once you do that, don't put out the creative fire by creating this false urgency on the data scientists. Don't stress them out because you wrongly believe you expect ROI in 6 months but you haven't seen it yet. It is a journey and a long-term play, so be prepared to wait a while for the value to surface, and it will surface in time.

Daniel Pears

Q1: What's your role exactly in the organization you are part of?

I'm the head of the UK Insights and Data practice at Capgemini, focusing on the financial services sector. This practice is a team of around 160 data professionals with domain knowledge in banking, capital markets, or insurance. Our data professionals cover a spectrum of expertise from your classic data engineering and platform development work, data management and data governance, data quality, and the teams of applied data services: data analytics, data visualization, etc. Also, [we have expertise in] regulatory programs, strategy, and consulting services.

Q2: How long have you acquired data science knowledge for?

I have a slightly different pathway [than other people in this role]; I was a statistician and an economist before I moved into technology, so I'd say that my data science expertise has come through about 10 years of experience of different types of data analytics. What clients are looking for in terms of data science these days is more of a spread. So, I've done things like primary data collection, statistical governance-style econometrics, customer or behavioral analytics, and that meant picking up technical skills like aggregate modeling, NLP, etc.

Q3: What's your domain expertise?

My main domain expertise is in customer analytics so I spent quite a bit of my career in marketing and campaign analytics in particular, and that lends itself to the customer or behavioral side of things as well.

Q4: What's the most important contribution of data science in your organization?

In my organization I think the most important contribution of data science is to augment behind-the-scenes kind of tasks, things like data integration, cloud, big data, and leveraging advanced data analytics in operational reporting. These are kind of an invisible art, something no one really notices. What data science can provide for my team is to provide a window to back-end operations work, and it exposes the technical elegance—or lack of!— of the architecture the business uses. It plays an incredibly important part in providing a window into how an organization manages its data. That's becoming a bigger requirement from my clients, in the sense that it's not just doing it, it's proving that you've done it.

Q5: What skills and attributes do you seek in a data scientist you hire?

I'll start with the easiest ones first. I'm looking for a degree of technical competence. I want people who have worked with industry standard tools, e.g. SAS, MATLAB, R Studio, and Python obviously, etc. That's the first pillar. I look for experience in different domains outside of financial services. It sounds quite strange since my team focuses solely on financial services, but what I find is data science is one of those fields where people who have had exposure in say consumer goods, transport, or telecommunications, they deal with different types of challenges that are really applicable to the financial services sector. I look for model diversity: regression modeling, linear processing, data visualization, etc. The more varied the style of algorithms or data science they've done, the more attractive a candidate they are. Lastly, the really great data scientists I've worked with bring an element of Art and Science combination; so, what they'll do is bring an attitude of curiosity or a degree of business exposure and context in the real world. These are the four things I look for in my ideal data science candidates. The technical skills are easy, but do they know how to deconstruct a problem; when a business user asks them, do they know how to pick the right model? If they only know one type of analysis, it's funny how all the problems are deconstructed towards that kind of analysis so it's important to be able to break the problem down from different perspectives. That quality is useful in all my consultants but in data science, it separates an average data scientist from a really great one.

Q6: How does AI fit in the whole data science work, in your domain?

That's an interesting one. [AI] is an overused term so I'm quite careful about how I use the term AI. AI is becoming an important part of discussions around data; what I'm not seeing with my more traditional-style data scientists is the understanding of how the feedback loop works in practice. In my team it is a new specialization that will have to emerge; and it's just not going to happen organically off the back of what people have done previously. There is an increased reliance on understanding the business process as a core underpinning of the AI development process, which I think a lot of my data scientists aren't familiar with. So, what I'm seeing is the emergence of the business analyst / data scientist or the hybridization of that role. If they really want to become good at the AI aspects of a solution, and AI is mimicking how a human would learn in the same context, if you don't understand that context, how would you design a machine [system] that would learn the same way?

Q7: What aspects of data science do you find most promising right now?

For me, there is a lot of noise about the customer space, but I don't think this is going to be the thing that is the transformation agent within the field. What I'm really interested in is how the resource-intensive processes that we have done in the past around conventional data delivery or data governance. I've seen some interesting things around how you almost get zero-person design zero-person build for commodity-based IT services. Things like how you build an ETL job without a human being needing to be involved, just using the AI to teach itself with data structures and semantic meaning, all based on data. A really killer app of AI in the next years would be something that would make the process behind the scenes work more efficiently. The customer stuff has been done to death (e.g. sentiment analysis) but there are a few interesting trends around a) customers becoming less comfortable with that and b) restricting access to that kind of processing. There is a much larger ethical consideration in that space as well which my clients are grappling with.

Q8: When do you find data science most relevant to a problem you are tackling?

That's quite an interesting question. I don't think I can give you a single answer. What I can do is talk about two or three thematic areas and work out the answer out of that. I see a lot of data science applications in things like routine customer-facing processes, e.g. routing communication to the right person and in particular things like complaints, which has been a big trend. This involves taking the text of the email or the waveform of the voice recording or the feed from the IVR and based on the analysis of how the person is speaking or what they are saying route it to a more experienced complaint manager. It's not so much about understanding the customer, so much as it is understanding the emotional context of their communications. The second thing I'm seeing is around the data quality and teaching a rules framework to teach itself. The reality of this is that it's a heavily rules-based discipline so what they are looking for is an AI that uses almost a classic brute-force technique as a precursor of something smarter. What I'm not seeing is people explicitly putting AI in front of the customer. There is a big misconception about AI being led by customer-facing processes in our industry—talking to the customer instead of a human being. Chatbots, for example, we are seeing focused more on inside organization communications—service desk requests, finding a file, etc. These tend to be the most relevant applications of AI.

Q9: How would you build a data science team?

It's an interesting challenge. I'll pre-warn you that my answer is still a hypothesis. We've tried a few different techniques in the past few years. The least elegant we did was hire a bunch of data scientists but what we realized was that the term data scientist covers 10-12 technical disciplines really and that hiring a NLP data scientist versus a machine learning data scientist and expecting them to do the same job is like hiring an oncologist and a cardiologist; they are both very skilled individuals and there is some common ground but they do very different jobs. We tried that and that didn't work, so what we ended up doing was hire a lead and let them pick the team. So we hired a very experienced data scientist. The problem is that the people who tend to be very good at these roles usually are not naturally people-people so it's very difficult to find people who are very good in data science but also good at a managerial role. So, that didn't quite work either. What we decided to do most recently and which seems to be the most promising [strategy] so far is building a team up around a project, understanding the disciplines of data science that you are looking at. So, for a project involving a lot of text, we go for an NLP data scientist. The second tier of all this is having to keep them in the organization once the project finishes. So what we have started doing is setting up laboratories within our practice so that they have something to work on while waiting for the next project. The big problem with Capgemini and with other professional services organizations is that data science projects tend to be quite short and sharp so they require a different operating model for these kinds of people (data scientists).

Q10: How do you gauge business acumen in a data science candidate?

We tend to test this through industry knowledge or scenarios. We use a lot of business case development work when we are doing our recruitment process. You're really looking for a couple of signals related to the degree of commerciality (e.g. understanding a trade-off between the good model and the perfect model), understanding the commercial drivers behind the questions being asked and why, what kind of decisions people will make based on the data, how long it's an acceptable time to run this analysis, whether the project is a long-term one or not, etc.

Q11: What process do you normally opt to automate or optimize through AI?

The main AI components we are seeing as targets for automation now tend to be things like on-boarding and Know Your Customer (KYC) processes for banks. That's related to targeting financial crime: things like anti-money-laundering, fraud, etc. where the core issue is knowing who is doing the transactions. Without exposing anyone in particular, a lot of the banks are not very good at knowing who their customers are, particularly the global ones where someone opens up an account in Mexico and they transfer money to the Philippines and then that money goes to Japan, etc. So, it's knowing not just the originating customer but the identities of all the different individuals involved. Up until now all these have been paper-driven— lots of paper being used—or multiple system hand-offs and the reality is that the data being used is not all that extensive. In terms of volume you're talking Kilobytes in most cases: SSN, customer name, postal address, swift code, etc. The problem is that because it's moving through so many parties, the data gets lost and updated and moved, and that kind of thing. We see a lot of focus on automating that because it cuts effort and time-to-market, as well as risk of the data being adjusted.

Q12: How relevant is domain knowledge for a data scientist in your area?

It depends on what level they are coming in at. When they first join my organization as junior data scientists I don't care so much about domain expertise. It's almost irrelevant because essentially they'll be working alongside someone more senior while they build their skills. That continues until they get to a level where they are decomposing a problem from a client. After that, you need to know what you are talking about, and certain industries are more sensitive than others. In some domains in financial services, the knowledge is important but not critical, while in other areas it becomes more essential.

Q13: What business processes do you find most relevant to data science work?

In the past it was like that but today more or less anything goes. The beauty of the field is that the frameworks and tools have evolved at the same level as the analytics tools. Where most of my data scientists are comfortable with is in the customer space but it's becoming cross-functional and [a] cross-organizational focus for most of my clients.

Q14: Which data science projects do you find yield the highest ROI?

This is almost a revisit of an earlier answer: the customer ones actually haven't and I see these stories of increased response rates by 300% but the original response rate was 0.01 and the cost of the algorithm development was probably higher. Where I've seen them make huge ROIs is those really unattractive things in the background, things like propensity to complain, with accuracy rates of about 80%. That was an incredibly high ROI and it was one of those things that didn't just do a one-off basic analysis, but built something that would change the business going forward. I've seen an email routing system that would half the number of people required to execute a trade. These projects related to background processes tend to have the highest ROI by far.

Q15: What advice would you give to data scientists, regarding the business aspect of things?

From a business engagement aspect I'd say that start with the business models first. The simple fact is the business understands how the business works and the closer you come to understanding it at their level the more elegant and more relevant your algorithms will become. In an AI context they won't work any other way. So, that business-first kind of mentality must be core to anyone joining the field these days; it's not a bonus, it's an expected capability.

Q16: What advice would you give to business people, regarding data science and AI?

I'd say the days of being opinion-rich and data-poor are over. The battle ground, particularly in my industry, over the next ten years is not going to be who can sell the lowest rate home loan, account, [or] policy, but who understands their products and customers better, and the context that they are making their decisions in. The threats are not coming from sideways, they are coming from below and above and all over the place, so from a business user in my field the product is data and basic data literacy is also going to become a fundamental requirement to anyone working in our industry for sure. It's not just about understanding statistics, but understanding how to interpret data in the business context is going to become a fundamental business skill as well. Everyone has to move a bit towards the data science field.

Reza Dilmaghani

Q1: What's your role exactly in the organization you are part of?

Leading the data science and analytics group in a consulting firm.

Q2: How long have you acquired data science expertise for?

Signal- and image-processing background. Overall ten years, including university.

Q3: What's your specialization in data science?

Event processing, with ANN background.

Q4: What's the most important contribution of data science / AI in your organization?

Wide range of application; reducing time and cost, automation.

Q5: What are the most important ways you add value to your organization through data science?

Figuring out solutions to business problems for various problems after framing them accordingly.

Q6: What's AI's role in all this, in your experience?

KYC, chatbots, identifying market trends, etc.

Q7: How do you remain relevant as a data scientist / AI professional these days?

Allocate some time to going to the university (King's College), Alan Turing Institute, and read or publish papers, [taking] one day a week.

Q8: What aspects of data science do you find most promising right now?

Trying to understand current practices and figuring out how data science can aid that, after understanding the business problems at hand. Communication and business liaising.

Q9: What are the key skills and qualities you find most useful in your data science work?

Data science has a very wide spectrum and the key skills and qualities depend on the domain mainly.

Q10: How do you know that an organization is data science-ready?

Having sufficient data that's also easily accessible. Having some procedures to share the data is immensely useful.

Q11: What kind of infrastructure does your organization have, in terms of data science?

Similar to the infrastructure of other organizations: evaluate the demand from the business side first.

Q12: What kind of business understanding differentiates you from a junior-level data scientist?

Having engagement with lots of businesses. Business acumen for understanding where the various tools are applicable. Experience. Broad understanding of what's going on in an organization or sector.

Q13: How relevant is domain knowledge these days when a Deep Learning system can bypass the feature engineering stage?

It's useful in the business side of the projects.

Q14: What are the key skills and qualities for a business stakeholder of a data science project?

General understanding of the data science buzzwords. Intelligence to see that there better ways to do a certain process, using data science. Being able to define the problem accurately.

Q15: What advice would you give to business people, regarding data science and AI?

No need to fear they will be replaced by an AI. Understand that we are trying to improve their efficiency and reduce costs through data science.

Q16: What advice would you give to data scientists, regarding the business aspect of things?

Shouldn't be one-dimensional; some understanding of the business practices is needed, at least some terminology.

Veysel Kocaman

Q1: What's your role exactly in the organization you are part of?

I'm the CTO and the head of A.I. so I have two roles: leading the software team to build the product and I also do the core AI features, like training the models, gathering the data, and coming up with the best approach and tools, like NLP.

Q2: How long have you acquired data science expertise for?

I started with data science in 2009 when I was done with my Master's thesis in Operations Research, so around ten years I think. Back then there were no plug-and-play tools or easy way to work with packages so I'd build an integration module by coding it myself.

Q3: What's your specialization in data science?

I have worked as an independent contractor solo for the last three years, I had to do everything by myself without any support from others so I had to work from data ingestion to deployment: the whole pipeline. So, my specialization is NLP, data engineering, and DevOps for machine learning. Right now, I work mostly with NLP and for my other projects, I also work on some regression models.

Q4: What's the most important contribution of data science or AI in your organization?

In this company, we try to connect job-seekers with their recruiters. Right now, there are many tools to make life easier for them but no one has touched the candidate side of the business. So, whenever our clients get a job offer email, we parse it with NLP and then we try to understand if the incoming email is a job description or not, and if that's the case we try to extract the job description part and convert it to an opportunity card, visible in the mobile app. Also, simple questions commonly asked by the recruiter are answered by our system which creates some predefined answers pulled from the user's records and answers the questions on behalf of the candidate.

Q5: What are the most important ways you add value to your organization through data science?

Every AI startup has a pitfall, like the cold-start problem, because in every closed domain, like a recruiting agency, we need to create our own training set. As we didn't have any data at first, my first suggestion was to gather as much domain-specific data as possible to be able to apply AI. Without [enough] data we cannot do AI. The second suggestion was to always include a human in the loop while working on the data, for example in labeling it. Instead of figuring out which unsupervised learning algorithm to use, it's best to inject humans inside for this task. The third one: the data scientist should be included into the team at the very beginning of each start-up, of each organization; if they don't integrate data science into their routine at the very beginning, they will not be able to collect the right data when they try to build some smart algorithms using AI.

Q6: What's AI's role in all this, in your experience?

We had some trouble while trying to generate some text to make it more natural, so AI came to play in all this. First, we need to understand the questions sent by the recruiters: that's natural language understanding, of course. By just using lookup labels, or parsing the data, we won't be able to understand that because it's not context-aware so there needs to be an NLU part and we also need some natural language generation part, but right now we don't have enough data for that. That's why we need to use some predefined text and use some placeholders by checking the database to find the answers, like from Text2SQL queries.

Q7: How do you remain relevant as a data scientist or AI professional these days?

First of all, every day I try to read at least five articles in my domain; anything of interest in this domain in medium.com or some forum, like Reddit. I keep myself updated with these articles. Sometimes it's just DevOps, like the Kubernetes, Docker or Airflow, sometimes it's just Quantum Computing—I just try to read without any particular intention. I always read, even if I don't memorize everything, and save the articles in my reading list, whenever I have some problem, or some idea to implement, this kind of previous reading will remind me what to look for and allow me to find the solution faster. Second of all, I listen to podcasts while driving or jogging. Every week I listen to at least two hours of podcasts. The third way [I remain relevant] is through mentoring. I always try to help the other people who try to switch into a data science career, I provide some pro-bono consultancy and free mentorship. The best way to keep updated is to teach. For example, I teach at the university once a week. I teach distributed data processing so I always need to keep myself updated and check the recent trends weekly. The fourth way would be through recruiting agencies when they call me and even though I'm not looking for a new job, I like to meet with them. I attend some meetups that they invite me as a speaker or a guest. I go there maybe once a month and I listen to what the other people are doing in the industry.

Q8: What aspects of data science do you find most promising right now?

Companies are still using human power to get some insights regarding the transaction of data. If [something] can be done by a human, it means that it can be automated, there is a pattern; if one single man can do that by himself and if he is good, we can imitate this with AI, a prediction model. The other thing is NLP. We are having an ImageNet moment in NLP at the moment and BERT-like architectures already beat human-level baselines. So I am really excited about what comes next in NLP and NLU.

Q9: What are the key skills and qualities you find most useful in your data science work?

I sometimes work with people who are unable to handle simple logic like for-loops; they are just building the models. And I also work with some people who are good at writing the code, but they cannot understand what the business problems are. So, the most important part of a data scientist is critical thinking. The first skill should be problem-solving through critical thinking and reasoning. The first step is the problem itself, the business problem. The second [step], is the data itself. So, data should be reliable as it's the biggest force multiplier in model building. Being able to clean the data properly, can be an important boost in a model's performance, since most of the time the data acquired is highly unstructured and even erroneous. The third step would be coding style. This is not just knowing the syntax but telling the computer how to solve the problem that you visualize in your mind. First, you need to solve the problem on paper. If you can solve it, you should be able to write code to solve it with computers. The fourth thing should be Statistics. Usually people say that Stats comes first, by looking at the data. It's important but not as high-priority as the other things, in my opinion. The fifth would be domain knowledge. This is when you work on some product or problem, you need to have some knowledge about what's going on under the hood in that business.

Q10: How do you know that an organization is data science-ready?

Sometimes it is the biggest headache if they don't have structured data and if they don't know what to do with the data, they hire data scientists just because of hype in the market. If they don't have any business problem that could be automated and they don't have data ready, they just rely on artificial data. Generally, they either produce garbage data or data bought from some vendors, which means they are not ready for data science yet. First, they need to start with some data collection before they hire any data scientists. If they don't have data, they cannot do any machine learning. Sometimes, their problems can be solved with some heuristics and data science is not magic, it's mathematics. So they first need to have some data that would represent their business or transactions. For the larger companies, in order to determine if they are data-centric, we need to see if their data is available, if their business problem can be solved with data instead of heuristics, if they already have some data collection, production, and enrichment pipeline, if they are using some structured (big) data architecture or if they just dump any data they collect. But if they don't have all [this], we'll have to spend (waste) a lot of time to get the data ready.

Q11: What kind of infrastructure does your organization have, in terms of data science?

We had no data at the beginning; we used someone's mailbox to understand the domain because in that mailbox most of the email transactions were job-related. This helped us understand what's needed and what could (or couldn't) be automated. Right now we keep track of our customers' every email being sent. Also, we are collecting all the transactions; when someone is rejected for a job opportunity, we collect the reason why, while we also let them rate the recruiters, etc. After dumping all the data in our data lakes, we retrain our models every once in a while to get better predictions and we always have some humans in the loop to intervene when needed till our AI models gets full-fledged.

Q12: What kind of business understanding differentiates you from a junior-level data scientist?

When junior-level data scientists solve a problem they focus on one aspect of that problem, the problem they have at that very moment. They are not very good at looking back and forward; that's the main problem. They are very bad at seeing the bigger picture. They just focus on getting the highest accuracy, forgetting everything else. When they focus on deployment, they forget about the accuracy. They just focus on the step they actually work on. Secondly, they are not good at problem-solving. They cannot code what they think, because they cannot solve the problem on paper. The third is that they don't understand the effects of their models in the business. I made the same mistake once. The businesses only focus on solving the problem they have, not the perfect accuracy of the prediction model. Experience cannot be replaced in that problem-solving skill.

Q13: How relevant is domain knowledge these days when a DL system can bypass the feature engineering stage?

The domain knowledge is very relevant and required during data preparation. If you don't know the inner aspects of the problem, if you don't talk with the people who are doing that business by hand, you don't understand the relationships among the features. Maybe they just look at three different features at the same time, so you should know that and discern which features are relevant and which aren't. You should understand the domain first. People are exaggerating the power of DL in terms of feature engineering but I insist that nothing can replace producing hand-crafted features devised by humans. Otherwise, we fail to mimic nature.

Q14: What are the key skills and qualities for a business stakeholder of a data science project?

They should understand that these are just decision support systems. They are not going to replace humans; they are there to help them make decisions. They shouldn't just rely on the outputs of our models. They should know that this is mathematics and statistics. This is the first thing they should be aware of. The second thing is that they shouldn't trust every good result. They should suspect it, because in the real world we cannot get 95% or 98% [accuracy] if we don't have enough data. Thirdly, they shouldn't trust the charts, if their data scientist or analyst is manipulating the charts. For example, when you get the predictions from the model, you can provide them a chart showing the best predictions of your current model and the worst ones of the previous model, on the same chart, to show improvement. This is cheating and a business person should question and check the data itself when in doubt. The last point would be that they shouldn't push for machine learning or AI if they don't have enough or reliable data.

Q15: What advice would you give to business people, regarding data science and AI?

They should focus more on data engineering, i.e. building a reliable data engineering pipeline so that they don't get stuck when building a data model. The second point would be that they should allocate role-specific people to certain roles; they shouldn't expect one data scientist to handle everything. For example, one person for DevOps, one for data engineering, an end-to-end data scientist (generalist) who can play with the data and moving it from the DB to the model-building part and an ML engineer who is good at model building and tuning. The fifth person would be a data analyst to handle daily querying and visualizations. If the company is already IT-oriented they would have this kind of person there already.

Q16: What advice would you give to data scientists, regarding the business aspect of things?

At first, they should understand the business problem, from the ground up. They should ask many questions and talk to many [relevant] people to understand the business process behind that data. Understand the domain they are working in. If they are in Agriculture, Finance, etc., they have many different aspects to focus more on. So, they need to keep up with their business transactions. Secondly, they should read anything that sounds interesting to them [related to data science]. For example, newsletters, forums, groups, and many daily digests and read anything they find, so that they can understand how other businesses are solving their problems so that they can imitate them for their own problems. Thirdly, they should be able to propose a new approach to solve some [business] problems and convey their ideas to business people involved. They should be curious all the time. Fourthly, they should be suspicious of good results, instead of being attracted by them. They shouldn't celebrate the early victories. When you know less, your self-confidence is high. That's a red flag. When you learn many things, the more you realize that you need to know more. Eventually, as you do that, you get some reliable self-confidence. You should always feel that "impostor syndrome" because it means that you are aware of your lack of competencies and that makes you hungrier to learn more things.

Chris Wright

Q1: How long have you been working as a data science / AI talent headhunter?

I've been working as a talent headhunter for well over ten years. I started looking into Big Data five years ago and then moved into data science and AI about four years ago when we decided to start a technical data science consultancy.

We still provide individual resources on a contract or full-time permanent basis, but also, we supply data science consulting services via our in-house team.

Q2: What's the demand like for data scientists these days?

So far in my career there always seems to be a demand for good data scientists.

There are a lot of people claiming to be data scientists in the marketplace but I would say someone who understands the nuances of business, is an excellent communicator, who has a mix of academic and real-world experience along with hands-on experience of the correct toolkits associated with modern data science should have no problem securing a job.

Q3: What's the demand like for AI professionals these days?

AI is a very broad subject so that's a hard question to answer. I would say if you are very good at something like deep learning, you are going to get snapped up by one of the big players: Google, Amazon or one of the other big players in this space.

There is also a demand across any number of startups who require 'Unicorn'- or 'Rockstar'- quality AI resources for their team. Alternatively, if you are that good, maybe you will create your own start-up business?

Q4: Why did you choose to specialize in this sort of roles in talent acquisition?

It's an exciting field to be in. You deal with very switched-on people, albeit it can be challenging sometimes.

Data science technologies span across every industry really. Data science can be applied in any industry where there are datasets and that's appealing to me as a businessman who's always looking to the future.

Because other technologies come and go, so you might be a specialist in one vertical market and that gets superseded by another technology suddenly making your brand and your entire [recruiting] database redundant.

Q5: What characteristics do you seek in a data scientist you approach for a given position?

Someone that I can ask to explain what they've done— with a customer, a data science project, etc., and explain to me coherently and I can understand it without taking all day. I'm not a data scientist but I do speak some of the lingo. Communication is key. Simplifying complicated problems and situations is one of the traits I have seen in people that I've placed. They can take almost anything, any subject or topic, and break it down into a simpler format. That mindset is invaluable in this space if you ask me.

Q6: What are the most common technical skills you encounter in data science jobs?

Obviously statistical packages, that's the core: R, Python, and now Julia. You are pretty much required to have one of those skills. Onwards from there, it depends on what kind of problems you are working on, what kind of datasets, as they are more domain-specific skills.

Q7: What are the most common soft skills you encounter in data science jobs?

Being able to listen, understand, and take onboard what the customer is saying. Not being arrogant.

Communication. It helps to be a social creature as a Data Scientist.

Q8: How much does a CV matter in data science and AI talent acquisition?

I think it matters a whole lot because the CV is the first thing someone is going to see. I've seen hiring managers look at a CV and say "I don't understand what's in this; it's poorly formatted, there are spelling mistakes in it, it's a no." If you can't take the care to format your CV and present it in a fashion that's coherent, what's to say that you are going to write a report well in the system you are working on. As a data scientist you should know how search engines react to the text of a CV, as well as how the reader will react to it too.

Q9: What platforms do you recommend for data science and AI professionals to use, when job-hunting?

I'd say stay clear off the so-called "specialist boards" and stick to the trusted ones. My favorite is the Jobsite board, which is also one of the busiest ones. If you are a contractor, put your CV in JobServe. LinkedIn is OK but you have to change your status there to show that you are looking for something else, as there are watchdogs who monitor this sort of activity and if they spot you they'll add you to a list if they are interested in your skill-set. My recommendation would always be to have a second phone number and not put your personal phone number on your CV. Turn that secondary number on when you are looking for work and you want the calls, and turn it off when you are working and you're happy because otherwise the flood of recruiters won't let you work or rest!

Q10: When is an organization data science-ready, in your view?

When the stakeholders understand the basics [of data science] and understand enough to see where value can be derived and to know that it's not just an instant solution.

Data Scientists and AI professionals tend to 'think differently.' I would say that the customer has to be coming to the table with an open mind and trying their best to understand and get into the data science mindset.

Q11: What kind of companies do you usually recruit data scientists and AI professionals for?

I have personally recruited Data Scientists for start-ups, consultancies, big four companies, asset managers, banks of different levels, and government, e.g. Ofgem.

Q12: How knowledgeable are the hiring managers of data science?

Some of them really know what they are talking about, and some, not so much. If their company is looking to invest in a Data Scientist, then they will usually have a firm idea of the capabilities or the goals they are trying to achieve with data science. The days of hiring a Data Scientist for the sake of hiring a Data Scientist or just because your competitor has one, seem to be passing and as the technology evolves, clients appear to gain more knowledge on the subject.

Q13: How detailed are the requirements for a data science or AI related position?

It depends on the complexity of the system, what the customer is trying to achieve. Also, it depends on whether a company wants to hire a data scientist because they think they should have one, versus someone who is building a very specific platform and who knows exactly what technologies are entailed. So, the specs are going to reflect that level of knowledge.

Q14: What advice would you give to business people, regarding data science and AI?

Book a consultation with Data Science Partnership!

Keep an open mind and find someone to advise you that gives you a 'warm fuzzy feeling'—a feeling of confidence that they understand your business and its objectives.

Look for someone who can simplify complexity who thinks outside the box. There are a lot of technologies out there and I can guarantee to you that however you are doing business now, there is a better way by exploiting data science.

Q15: What advice would you give to data scientists, regarding the business aspect of things?

Try and understand as much as you can about the running of a business and gain as much business acumen as you can.

Try to look at things from an 'operational' standpoint.

Don't be arrogant and focus on being part of a team.

Glossary

A

Agile Methodology: a project management process that emphasizes dividing projects into several small stages and the incremental enhancement of the solutions.

Algorithm: a step-by-step procedure for calculations and logical operations. In an AI setting, algorithms can be designed to facilitate machine learning and acquire knowledge by themselves, rather than relying on hard-coded rules.

Application Programming Interface (API): a set of definition, protocols, tools, and routines for interacting with a program, usually via the Internet. APIs are essential for linking programming languages to various frameworks like deep learning ones.

Artificial Intelligence (AI): a field of computer science dealing with the emulation of human intelligence using computer systems and its applications to a variety of domains. AI application in data science is noteworthy and has been an important factor in the field since the 2000s.

Artificial Neural Network (ANN): a graph-based artificial intelligence system, implementing the universal approximator idea. Although ANNs have started as a machine learning system, focusing on predictive analytics, they have expanded over the years to include a large variety of tasks. ANNs comprise a series of nodes called neurons, which are organized in layers. The first layer corresponds to all the inputs, the final layer to all the outputs, and the intermediary layers to a series of meta-features the ANN creates, each having a corresponding weight. ANNs are stochastic in nature so every time they are trained over a set of data, the weights are noticeably different.

B

Big data: an area of computer science that is interested in the efficient processing and storage of very large amounts of data. Although definitions of the term vary from person to person, one can succinctly define big data as the amount of data that is big enough so that an average personal computer is unable to process it.

Business intelligence (BI): a sub-field of data analytics focusing on basic data analysis of business-produced data, for the purpose of improving the function of a business. BI is not the same as data science though.

Business question: a case of lack of information or clarity on a given business problem. Oftentimes, data science can help provide this information through the analysis of the relevant data and the synthesis of the outcomes into actionable insights.

C

Chatbot: an artificial intelligence system that emulates a person in a chat application. A chatbot takes as its inputs text, processes it in an efficient manner, and yields a reply in text format. A chatbot may also carry out simple tasks, based on its inputs and it can reply with a question in order to clarify the objective involved.

Classification: a very popular data science methodology, under the predictive analytics umbrella. Classification aims to solve the problem of assigning a label (a.k.a. class) to a data point, based on pre-existing knowledge of categorized data, available in the training set.

Classifier: a predictive analytics system geared towards classification problems.

Cloud (computing): a paradigm that enables easy, on-demand access to a network of shareable computing resources that can be configured and customized to the application at hand. The cloud is a very popular resource in large-scale data analytics and a common resource for data science applications.

Clustering: a data science methodology involving finding groups in a given dataset, usually using the distances among the data points as a similarity metric. In marketing, sometimes known as segmentation.

Computer Vision: an application of artificial intelligence, where a computer is able to discern a variety of visual inputs and effectively "see" a lot of different real-world objects in real-time. Computer vision is an essential component of all modern robotics systems.

D

Data analytics: a general term to describe the field involving data analysis as its main component. Data analytics is more general than data science, although the two terms are often used interchangeably.

Data anonymization: the process of changing the data so that it cannot be used to identify any particular individual. This involves removing or masking any personal identified information from the data analyzed.

Data engineering: the part of the data science pipeline where data is acquired, cleaned, and processed, so that it is ready to be used in a data model. Most artificial intelligence systems handle a large part of the data engineering once they are given the data that we want them to model.

Data exploration: the part of the data science pipeline where the various variables are examined using statistics and data visualization, in order to understand various qualities of the data better and work out best approaches for the stages that follow.

Data model: a data science module processing or predicting some piece of information, using existing data, after the latter has been pre-processed and made ready for this task. Data models add value and are comprised of non-trivial procedures. In AI, data models are usually sophisticated systems making use of several data-driven processes under the hood.

Data science: the interdisciplinary field undertaking data analytics work on all kinds of data, with a focus on big data, for the purpose of mining insights or building data products.

Data science question: a case of lack of information related to a given data science problem, usually linked to a hypothesis or experiment. Data science questions are often linked to business questions since they are driven by the latter.

Data visualization: the process of creating visuals based on the original data, or the data stemming from the data model built using the original data.

Dataset: the data available to be used in a data analytics project, in the form of a table or a matrix. A dataset may need some work before it is ready for use in a data model, though in many artificial intelligence models, you can use it as is.

Deep Learning (DL): an artificial intelligence methodology, employing large artificial neural networks, to tackle very complex problems. DL systems require a lot of data in order to yield a real advantage in terms of performance.

Dimensionality reduction: the process of reducing the number of features in a dataset, usually through the merging of the original features in a more compact form (feature fusion), or through the discarding of the less information-rich features (feature selection).

E

Ensemble: "The process by which multiple models, such as classifiers or experts, are strategically generated and combined to solve a particular computational intelligence problem. Ensemble learning is primarily used to improve the (classification, prediction, function approximation, etc.) performance of a model, or reduce the likelihood of an unfortunate selection of a poor one" (adapted from Dr. Robi Polikar). Ensembles may also involve AI systems too, such as optimizers, in order to attain a better performance than a single such system.

Ethics: a code of conduct for a professional. In data science, ethics involves certain practices like data security, privacy, and proper handling of the insights derived from the data analyzed.

ETL (Extract, Transform and Load): a process in all data-related pipelines, with the purpose of pulling data out of the source systems (usually databases) and placing it into a data warehouse or a data governance system. ETL is an important part of data acquisition, preceding any data modeling efforts.

F

Feature: a processed variable capable of being used in a data science model. Features are generally the columns of a dataset.

Feature engineering: the process of creating new features, either directly from the data available, or via the processing of existing features. Feature engineering is part of data engineering in the data science process.

Feature selection: the data science process according to which the dimensionality of a dataset is reduced through the selection of the most promising features and the discarding of the less promising ones. How promising a feature is depends on how well it can help predict the target variable and is related to how information-rich it is.

Fitness function: an essential part of most artificial intelligence systems, particularly optimization-related ones. It depicts how close the system is getting to the desired outcome and helps it adjust its course accordingly. In most AI systems the fitness function represents an error or some form of cost, which needs to be minimized, though in the general case it can be anything and depending on the problem, it may need to be maximized.

Framework: a set of tools and processes for developing, testing, and deploying a certain system. Most AI systems today are created using a framework. A framework is usually accompanied by a library/package in the programming languages it supports. In the deep learning case, for example, a framework can be a programming suite like MXNet, that enables a variety of deep learning related processes and classes to be utilized.

G

Generalization: a key characteristic of a data science model, where the system is able to handle data beyond its training set in a reliable way. A proxy to good generalization is similar performance between the training set and a testing set, as well as consistency among different training-testing set partitions of the whole dataset.

Graph: a kind of dimensionless structure that is an abstraction of the objects involved in a process as well as their relationships, their connections. It is characterized by nodes and arcs, representing the objects and the connections respectively. The latter also carry other characteristics too, such as weights, corresponding to the strength of each connection.

Graph analytics: a data science methodology making use of graph theory to tackle problems through the analysis of the relationships among the entities involved.

I

IDE (Integrated Development Environment): a system designed for facilitating the creation and running of scripts as well as their debugging. Jupyter is a popular IDE for data science applications.

Insight: a non-obvious and potentially useful piece of information derived from the use of a data science model on some data.

Interpretability: the ability to more thoroughly understand a data model's outputs and derive how they relate to its inputs (features). Lack of interpretability is an issue for deep learning systems.

J

Julia: a modern programming language of the functional programming paradigm, comprising characteristics for both high-level and low-level languages. Its ease of use, high speed, scalability, and sufficient amount of packages, make it a robust language well-suited for data science.

After v. 1.0 of the language was released in the summer of 2018, it has been officially production-ready.

Jupyter: a popular browser-based IDE for various data science languages, such as Python and Julia.

K

Kaggle: a web site that hosts data science competitions and provides many useful datasets.

M

Machine Learning (ML): a set of algorithms and programs that aim to process data without relying on statistical methods. ML is generally faster and some methods of it are significantly more accurate than the corresponding statistical ones, while the assumptions made about the data are fewer. There is a noticeable overlap between ML and AI systems designed for data science.

Mapping: the process of connecting a variable or a set of variables to a variable we are trying to predict (i.e. the target variable). Mappings can be analytical using a mathematical function or not, such as employing a set of rules, or a network of functions, as in the case of an artificial neural network. Mappings are inherent in every data model.

Meta-features (a.k.a. super features or synthetic features): high quality features that encapsulate larger amounts of information, usually represented in a series of conventional features. Meta-features are either synthesized in an artificial intelligence system, or created through certain dimensionality reduction algorithms.

Methodology: a set of methods and the theory behind those methods, for solving a particular kind of problem in a certain field. Methodologies of data science include classification, regression, etc. while for artificial intelligence, we have methodologies like deep learning, autoencoders, etc.

Model Maintenance: the process of updating or even upgrading a data model as new data becomes available or as the assumptions of the problem change.

MXNet: a deep learning framework developed by Apache. MXNet is linked to Amazon, although it can run on any cloud service. Its main API is called Gluon and it's part of the main package of MXNet. There are several such packages in different programming languages, each one an API for that language. MXNet can support more programming languages than any other AI framework.

N

Natural Language Processing (NLP): a text analytics methodology focusing on categorizing the various parts of speech for a more in-depth analysis of the text involved.

O

Optimization: an artificial intelligence process, aimed at finding the best value of a function (usually referred to as the fitness function) given a set of restrictions. Optimization is key in all modern data science systems. Although there are deterministic optimization algorithms out there, most of the modern algorithms are stochastic.

Optimizer: a (usually AI-based) system designed to perform optimization.

Overfitting: the case wherein a model is too specialized to a particular dataset. Its main characteristic is great performance for the training set and poor performance for any other dataset. Overfitting is a characteristic of an overly complex model.

P

Personally Identifiable Information (PII): information that can be used to pinpoint a particular individual, thereby violating his/her privacy. PII is an important ethical concern in data science and may not be so easy to tackle, since it often relies on combinations of variables.

Pipeline: also known as workflow, it is a conceptual process involving a variety of steps, each one of which can comprise several other processes. A pipeline is essential for organizing the tasks needed to perform any complex procedure (often non-linear) and is very applicable in data science—this application is known as the data science pipeline.

Predictive analytics: a set of methodologies of data science, related to the prediction of certain variables. It includes a variety of techniques such as classification, regression, time-series analysis, and more. Predictive analytics are a key part of data science.

Python: a widely used object-oriented programming language, typically used for data science, as well as artificial intelligence applications geared towards data analytics.

R

Regression: a very popular data science methodology, under the predictive analytics umbrella. Classification aims to solve the problem of predicting the values of a continuous variable corresponding to a set of inputs, based on pre-existing knowledge of similar data, available in the training set.

Regressor: a predictive analytics system geared towards regression problems.

Return on Investment (ROI): a popular metric in business, for assessing how good an investment is. Positive values are generally good, while the higher the value, the better. ROI is usually expressed as a percentage.

S

Sample: a limited portion of the data available, useful for building a model, and ideally representative of the population it belongs to.

Sampling: the process of acquiring a sample of a population using a specialized technique. Sampling is very important to be done properly to ensure that the resulting sample is representative of the population studied. Sampling needs to be random and unbiased.

Scala: a functional programming language, very similar to Java, that is used in data science. The big data framework Spark is based on Scala.

Scrum framework: is a framework within the set of Agile methodologies which targets effective team collaboration on complex products.

Sentiment analysis: a natural language processing method involving the classification of a text into a predefined sentiment, or solving for a numeric value that represents sentiment polarity—that is, how positive or how negative the overall sentiment is.

Supervised learning: a set of data science methodologies where there is a target variable that needs to be predicted. The main parts of supervised learning are classification, regression, and reinforcement learning.

T

Target variable: the variable of a dataset that is the target of a predictive analytics system, such as a classification or a regression system.

TensorFlow: a deep learning and high performance numerical computation library. Initiated by Google and improved by a very large open source community, TensorFlow is by far the most popular deep learning framework today.

U

Unsupervised learning: a set of data science methodologies where there is no target variable that needs to be predicted.

V

Variable: a column in a dataset, be it in a matrix or a dataframe. Variables are usually turned into features, after some data engineering is performed on them.

W

Workflow: see pipeline.

Index

www.ingramcontent.com/pod-product-compliance
Lightning Source LLC
Chambersburg PA
CBHW071241050326
40690CB00011B/2216